Practical

Elemental

Magick

Published by Avalonia

BM Avalonia
London
WC1N 3XX
England, UK

www.avaloniabooks.co.uk

PRACTICAL ELEMENTAL MAGICK

ISBN (10) 1-905297-19-X
ISBN (13) 978-1-905297-19-1

First Edition October 2008
Copyright © 2008 Sorita d'Este and David Rankine

Design by Satori.

Practical

Elemental

Magick

Working the Magick of the Four Elements in the Western Mystery
Tradition

David Rankine & Sorita d'Este

"For those who wish to devote themselves to this science,
it is important that they believe with conviction in the Spirits,
who are free from base and worldly matters.
The Cabalist sages have called them
Gnomes, Sylphs, Salamanders and Nymphs,
and they have extraordinary powers
to do quite remarkable things,
when you request them to do so with the
appropriate ceremonies."

The Keys of Rabbi Solomon, Wellcome MS 4670, 1796

ABOUT THE AUTHORS

Sorita d'Este & David Rankine are students and practitioners of the Western Esoteric Tradition who live and work in Wales (UK). Between them they have authored and contributed to more than 30 books on subjects related to mythology, magick and spirituality. This book *"Practical Elemental Magick"* was written to compliment their very popular *"Practical Planetary Magick"* published in 2006.

Both Sorita and David have lectured extensively on a wide range of esoteric subjects and have facilitated workshops throughout the UK and Europe. Since 2000 they have been working together in what has been a very fruitful and colourful partnership, producing not only projects such as this, but also a beautiful baby boy. In their writing and other work together they draw from their experience in a number of traditions, with their extensive research on a wide range of western esoteric subjects including Qabalah, the grimoire traditions, Classical Paganism of Greece, Rome and Egypt, British and other *"Celtic"* mythologies.

You are welcome to write to the authors:

Sorita d'Este & David Rankine
c/o BM Avalonia, London, WC1N 3XX, England, UK

Table of Contents

Elemental Magick 11

The Four Elements 16

    Air - Works of Knowledge 21

    Fire - Works of Will 25

    Water – Works of Daring 29

    Earth – Works of Silence 33

Elemental Interaction 36

    Elemental Body Meditation 40

Exploring the Elements 42

    Air Meditation 42

    Flame Meditation 43

    Living Water Meditation 44

    Silent Earth Meditation 46

The Unification Rite 47

    The Unification Rite of the Four Elements............49

The Elemental Archangels 52

    The Archangel of Air - Raphael 55

    The Archangel of Fire - Michael............................56

    The Archangel of Water - Gabriel 57

    The Archangel of Earth - Uriel 58

The Elemental Beings..60

    The Elemental Rulers..64

    Classification of Elemental Beings 66

    Sylphs of Air 71

    Salamanders of Fire 74

Undines of Water 76

Gnomes of Earth 78

Elemental Tides 80

Preparation for Ritual 83

The Elemental Tools 87

Dagger 87

Wand 88

Pentacle 90

Cup 91

Altar..92

Elemental Tool Consecration.................................94

The Magick Circle of the Four Elements 96

Creating your Elemental Circle..............................97

The Elemental Pyramids...100

The Air Pyramid..102

The Fire Pyramid...105

The Water Pyramid..108

The Earth Pyramid...111

The Pyramid of Aether...114

The Elemental Temples 118

Temple: Inwards & Outwards................................119

Temple: The Four Winds..120

Temple: Flame 121

The Water Temple..122

The Earth Temple..122

The Inner Talisman 124

Invocation of the Archangels....................................126

Elementaries...137

Creation of an Elementary....................................140

The Elemental Deities **142**

   The Air Gods 144

   The Fire Gods 146

   The Water Gods..148

   The Earth Gods...150

APPENDIX

Four or Three plus One? 154

Symbols of the Four Elements....................................157

Elemental Fragrances 158

The Elements and Minerals 159

The Elements and Plants...161

The Elements and Animals..162

Names of Power...164

Intonation of Words of Power......................................165

License to Depart 167

The Pentagram 168

Other Systems of Elements 172

Elements in the Zodiac..174

Dealing with Vexatious Elementals.............................176

Terms and Definitions...179

Bibliography **181**

Dedicated to the Alumni of the O.I.F.
The Light of Truth burns with an ineffable flame.

CHAPTER 1

Elemental Magick

"The number and the nature of those things,
Called elements, what Fire, Earth, Air forth brings;
From whence the heavens their beginnings had;
Whence tide, whence rainbow in gay colours clad,
What makes the clouds that gathered are, and black,
To send forth lightning, and a thundering crack;
What doth the nightly flames, and comets make;
What makes the Earth to swell, and then to quake:
What is the seed of metals, and of gold
What virtues, wealth, doth Nature's coffer hold..."[1]

The four elements of Air, Fire, Water and Earth exist as spiritual essences, as philosophical concepts, as energy states and as a tangible physical reality. When we work with the elements we are returning to the building blocks of magick, rooting our feet in the physical world to effect positive change, whether that be in our psyches, our lives or our environment.

Because of their immediate and solid presence in the natural world, the four elements are the simplest forces to work magick with. However, this simplicity does not indicate a lack of power, rather it is a

---

1 Three Books of Occult Philosophy, Book I, Ch. 2, Agrippa

tangible purity of being which we can touch and learn to control. In mastering the four elements within and without we master ourselves, bringing the external forces of the natural world and the internal forces of our existence into harmony.

The power of the four elements can be seen implicitly in the pantheons of the earliest civilizations, in deities of sea and Moon, Sun and flame, Earth and wind. This association of deities with the four elements was formalised in the fifth century BCE, in the writings of the Greek philosopher and magician Empedocles. In his work *Tetrasomia*, Empedocles wrote:

> *"Now hear the fourfold Roots of everything:*
> *Enlivening Hera, Aidoneus, bright Zeus,*
> *And Nestis, moistening mortal springs with tears."*[2]

We can see the awesome destructive power of the elements when they are isolated (or out of balance), such as a tidal wave, earthquake or forest fire. This emphasis on the power of the elements demonstrates a simple truth about them, which is their physical reality. Unlike other forms of magick, elemental magick draws on powers which are immediately to hand. Our world, and everything on it, is made up of the four elements.

Wherever we travel on the face of the earth, if we are on land we are in touch with the element of earth. Likewise we are always in touch with the element of air, which surrounds us and keeps us alive. We are rarely far from water, whether it be the sea, a river, or even the piping which brings water into the home. Fire is also nearby, but in a slightly different way. Natural fire is beneath the earth, in the molten core within the planet, and the lava which spews out of volcanoes

---

2 Tetrasomia, Empedocles, C5th BCE.

when they erupt. Fire can be created in the strike of a match or by many other methods. So when we perform elemental magick, we draw on forces which are always in contact with us (air and earth), or are easily located or collected (water) or created (fire).

Working with the four elements is the foundation of practical magick. Learning to understand the qualities and powers of the four elements enables the magician to recognise their presence in the different parts of their being, from the physical to the emotional, mental and spiritual. This is followed by focusing the will to control and direct the power of the elements, a skill which develops through experience and understanding gained in practice.

The use of elemental energy may range from the powering of charms or sigils and the charging of spells, to the transformation of the psyche, and the creation of elementaries (thought-forms). In the past forms of the four elements were also commonly used for other purposes such as being the physical mediums for divination. Each of the elements has associated qualities making them particularly suited to magick with specific applications, so for example when creating a talisman or ritual to improve fertility the best element to work with would be the element of Earth, or to ensure exam success the most suitable element would be Air.

The table that follows contains a number of intentions with the most appropriate element for each. You should consult this list at the beginning of the process of qualifying your intent to help you focus on refining your purpose in the most effective way. Please note that in some instances there is more than one suitable element and in such instances we cite all those suitable.

Additionally, you may find that you need to combine correspondences, or choose between the most suitable elements to work with in some instances. By working with the elements you will develop an instinctual *"feel"* for each in time and should be able to add any additional personal correspondences or intentions you feel appropriate to this table.

Table of Intentions

Intention	Element
Ambition, development of	Air
Anger, controlling	Fire
Astral Travel	Water
Attraction, increasing	Earth
Beauty, developing	Earth
Birth, safely	Water
Business success	Air
Career success	Fire; Air
Clairvoyance, developing	Water
Communication, improving	Air
Courage, enhancing	Fire
Creativity, increasing	Air, Fire
Discord, causing	Fire
Discord, preventing	Air
Dreams, promoting & remembering	Water; Air
Duty, performing	Earth
Energy, increasing	Fire
Enthusiasm, increasing	Air
Equilibrium, establishing	Earth
Ethics, developing	Air
Examination success	Air
Fear, dispelling	Fire
Fertility, increasing	Earth
Flexibility, developing	Air
Fortune, improving	Air
Friendship, developing	Earth
Future, learning the	Air; Water
Glamour, developing	Water
Harmony, developing	Fire; Air
Healing, giving	Fire; Air
Health, improving	Air
Home, protecting	Earth

Honour, acquiring	Air
Humour, improving	Air
Illusions, creating	Water
Illusions, dispelling	Earth
Influence, developing	Air
Journey, protection	Air (air); Water (sea) ; Earth (land)
Knowledge, increasing	Air
Law, dealing with	Air; Earth
Leadership, developing	Fire
Love, obtaining or promoting	Earth ; Water
Luck, improving	Air
Lust, satisfying	Earth; Fire
Memory, improving	Air
Money, acquiring	Fire
Music, learning or improving	Air
Passion, increasing	Fire; Earth
Patience, developing	Earth
Patronage, obtaining	Fire
Peace, establishing	Fire; Air
Pleasure, ensuring	Earth
Practicality, developing	Earth
Promotion, gaining	Fire; Air
Property, recovering	Air
Public speaking, successfully	Air
Responsibility, taking	Air; Water
Self-confidence, increasing	Earth
Self-confidence, developing	Earth
Sex-drive, decreasing	Earth
Sex-drive, increasing	Fire
Social skills, improving	Earth; Air
Strength, increasing	Fire; Earth
Teaching, developing	Earth; Air
Truth, learning or promoting	Air
Unconscious, accessing	Water
Vigour, increasing	Fire
Wealth, improving	Fire; Earth
Willpower, strengthening	Fire

CHAPTER 2

The Four Elements

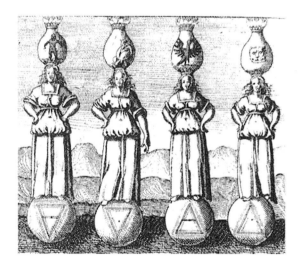

"For he hath given me certain knowledge of the things that are, namely, to know how the world was made, and the operation of the elements."[3]

Once established, the fourfold system of the elements became the foundation for the western traditions of magick, and also influenced the spirituality of the developing religions. Whilst the influence of the four elements on religion has decreased over the centuries, the

---

3 The Wisdom of Solomon 7:17, C4th CE.

converse is true with magick, and the four elements have become, if anything, even more important in the practice of magick. This is largely due to the fact that the four elements represent the building blocks of form and the transformative actions of force.

The origins of the four elements as a complete system can be found in the writings of the ancient Greek philosopher Empedocles in the fifth century BCE. In his *Tetrasomia* (*Doctrine of the Four Elements*), Empedocles expressed the view that the four elements were not only the building blocks of the universe, but also spiritual essences. He equated the sources of the elements to deities, giving divine origins to the elements.

We must note that Empedocles did not call his four principles *'elements'* (*stoikheia*), but rather he used the terms *'roots'* (*rhizai*) and *'root-clumps'* (*rhizômata*). Empedocles was an herbal magician or root cutter (*rhizotomoi*) and created his theory in the process of developing a doctrine of occult sympathies in plants. Other great philosophers subsequently applied themselves to the clarification and expansion of this doctrine. Aristotle in the fourth century BCE expounded further on the elements as spiritual essences, concentrating on their qualities in his work *De Generatione et Corruptione*. A few decades later, in his *Timaeus*, Plato postulated a different view of the four elements, suggesting that the elements were instead changeable as manifested qualities of the primary matter of the universe.

The Stoics held a different view of the four elements, attributing only one quality each to them rather than the two suggested by Empedocles, Aristotle and Plato. They declared *"Fire is the hot element, water the moist, air the cold, earth the dry."*[4] These two somewhat different views would between them influence the early Christian

---

4 Vitae, Diogenes Laertius, C3rd CE.

theologians like Athenagoras, Aristides and Eusebius and Jewish philosophers like Philo and Josephus. Even though both schools of thought were influential, and permeated the views of the time, they did not go off on the tangent seen in Gnosticism, where the elements were divided into good and evil.

The Christian view of the body put forward by the early Christian theologians was that it was comprised of the four elements with the fifth element (aether) being the animating soul. This Christian view is very much the one which would continue through the centuries into the western esoteric traditions and the various schools of magick working within it.

Returning to the Greek views of the elements, in the third century BCE the Ptolemaic Egyptian high priest and historian Manetho recorded deity attributions which seem to almost sit as a bridge between the ideas of Empedocles and those of later traditions.

"The Egyptians say that Isis and Osiris are the Moon and the Sun; that Zeus is the name which they give to the all-pervading Spirit, Hephaestus to Fire, and Demeter to Earth. Among the Egyptians the moist element is named Oceanus and their own river Nile; and to him they ascribed the origin of the Gods. To Air, again, they give, it is said, the name of Athena."[5]

Philolaos, the fifth century BCE Pythagorean philosopher wrote on the fourfold ordering of the elements to the four segments of the zodiacal circle. This may have been the first association of the circle in quarters with the elements, and also emphasises the symbolic relevance of the symbol for planet Earth, being a circle with an equal-armed cross dividing it into four quarters. These four quarters thus equate to the four elements which the planet is comprised of.

---

5 Manetho, Aegyptica Fragment 83, Waddell (trans), C2nd BCE.

Element	Fire	Air	Water	Earth
Dominant Quality	Warm	Moist	Cool	Dry
Secondary Quality	Dry	Warm	Moist	Cool
Nature	Active	Active	Passive	Passive
	Light	Light	Heavy	Heavy
	Ascending	Ascending	Descending	Descending
Movement	Upwards	Upwards	Downwards	Downwards
		Sideways	Sideways	

The Pythagoreans associated the elements with the natural cycle, tying the qualities of the elements to the seasons of plant growth. Thus we see the process beginning with Moisture, the spring rains which encourage rapid growth, producing the green shoots as plants grow towards the sun. This leads to the second phase of Warmth, where the summer sun encourages growth (through photosynthesis) to maturity. The third phase is Dryness, the leaves of autumn and the stiffening of stems. Finally the fourth phase is Cool, the chills of winter, death and retreat into the earth ready for the cycle to begin again.

This relationship between the four elements and the four qualities was well known, and is clearly illustrated in Simon Forman's sixteenth century alchemical work *Of the Division of Chaos:*

"Then out of this Chaos, the four elements were made:
Heat and cold, moist and dry, in like wise,
Which are the beginning of all creatures wide,
That under the globe of Luna do abide."

The Greek spiritual alchemist Zosimos of Panopolis attributed the elements to the four cardinal points in his classic third century CE work *Upon the Letter Omega.* The attribution of the four elements to the four directions remained constant for many centuries, with Fire in the east, Air in the south, Water in the west and Earth in the north. This can be seen through to at least the eighteenth century, where the *Key of Solomon* records that, *"the spirits created of fire are in the East and those of the winds in the South."*[6]

It would be Eliphas Levi in the mid nineteenth century with his writings who clearly switched the attributions of Air and Fire, giving Air as being attributed to the East and Fire to the South.

It must be borne in mind that the special kingdom of Gnomes is at the north, that of the Salamanders at the south, that of Sylphs at the east, and that of Undines at the west."[7]

This attribution was picked up by the Hermetic Order of the Golden Dawn, and has become the standard attribution in nearly all of the Western Esoteric Traditions.

---

6 Key of Solomon (various MSS).

7 Transcendental Magic, Levi.

Air - Works of Knowledge

*"People and other animals live by breathing air,
and this is for them both soul and intelligence."*[8]

Axiom	To Know
Colour (Modern)	Yellow, Sky Blue
Astrological Signs	Aquarius, Gemini, Libra
Planets	Jupiter*, Mercury (Uranus)
Direction	East or South
Time of Day	Dawn
Season	Spring
Sense	Smell
Gender	Masculine
Tools	Wand
Deities	Zeus
Tetragrammaton	Vav
Archangel	Raphael
Demon King	Oriens
Enochian King	Bataivah
Enochian Divine Name	Oro Ibah Aozpi
Elemental Governor	Cherub
Elemental King	Paralda
Elementals	Sylphs
Kerub	Eagle
Gem	Topaz
Metal	Silver, Tin
Tarot	Swords
Platonic Solid	Octahedron

---

8 Diogenes of Apollonia, C5th BCE.

Some philosophers, such as the sixth century BCE Greek philosopher Anaximenes, believed that everything came from Air. He wrote of Air that:

"Air differs in essence in accordance with its rarity or density. When it is thinned it becomes fire, while when it is condensed it becomes wind, then cloud, when still more condensed it becomes water, then earth, then stones. Everything else comes from these."[9]

Air is an analytical masculine element, associated with the word (logos). From this it is easy to see why it should be connected with logic and the intellect, the power of thought and the gathering of knowledge. This is why the axiom of Air is *To Know*, and of course with that knowledge comes the need to communicate, and so language and sound, which travel through the Air, are also implied. With knowledge comes the ability to learn and improve skills, and these qualities are also airy. Another quality of Air is clarity, the ability to perceive clearly, analyse the facts and then exercise discernment, i.e. informed choice based on knowledge. It is associated with the quality of discrimination, and the ability to analyse, to see the whole picture with a *'birds-eye view'*, and the wisdom of experience.

Memory is another airy quality, and it is no coincidence that the sense of smell, recognizing scents carried on the Air, should be known as the *'evoker of memory'* due to its ability to prompt memories more than any other sense.

Air has been connected with the soul in many cultures, and this is seen particularly in the Western magickal languages, with examples such as *Ruach* (Hebrew) meaning *'spirit'*, *'breath'* or *'wind'*; *Psyche* (Latin) is derived from *psukhê* (Greek) meaning *'breath'*, *'life'* or *'soul'*;

---

9 DK13A5 in the Diels-Kranz Collection.

and *Pneuma* (Greek) meaning *'breath'*, *'soul'* or *'vital spirit'*. The breath of life is a universal concept and as such it is no surprise that it should be accorded such significance.

The creative logos is implicit in the breath of life – *in principio erat verbum*.[10] The idea of the word or breath creating the universe is seen in various pantheons, such as with the Egyptian magick god Thoth speaking the word of creation. The power of words is extreme, with them you can describe something, and create an image for another person's imagination, hence the pen truly being mightier than the sword. Likewise the power inherent in the true name being considered able to control that thing, hence the importance of not revealing the true name, and the tale of the Egyptian goddess Isis learning the creator sun god Re's true name through subterfuge to make herself the mistress of magick.

In the macrocosm Air is most obvious as the sky, and felt in the winds that blow around us. As the most intangible of the four elements, Air connects us to the stars, filling the gap between the Earth and the heavens. Air surrounds us at all times, the omnipresent breath of life, continually energizing us as we draw oxygen from it to keep our bodies working and vitalize ourselves.

Air is associated with inspiration, a term which can literally mean to breathe in. When we are inspired ideas move in our minds, and movement is a quality of Air, as seen in nature by the power of the wind, which can vary from a gentle breeze to a raging tornado, demonstrating its changeability. Air also embodies joy and happiness, the lightness of spirit you feel when you are in a good mood. Feeling happy is often described as *'floating on air'*. Air brings beginnings, like the tide of air which starts the year in spring. Air embodies the hope

---

10 In the Beginning was the Word – John 1.1

of a spring day, the clarity of a sharp intake of breath, the joy of a cooling breeze, the freedom of a bird gliding on the winds.

The alchemical acronym for air, using the Greek word *aer*, is *Aurifica Ego Regina*, meaning "*I, the Gold-making Queen.*" This refers to the seduction of Danaë by Zeus (the air god) as a golden shower in Greek myth.

Working with the element of Air enables you to concentrate on your mental being, enhancing your mind and its capabilities from the intellect, clarity and memory to inspiration, knowledge and its analysis. This enhancement may also be applied to the learning process, be it to learn new languages, skills or crafts, or pass exams.

As the spoken word it also enables development of the social being, both through improving communication and also by transforming the negative mental states which can inhibit effective socialisation, such as anxiety, indecision, insecurity, nervousness and paranoia.

Qualities (positive)	Analysis, Clarity, Communication, Decisiveness, Discrimination, Élan, Grace, Happiness, Heaven, Hope, Intellect, Inspiration, Joy, Justice, Knowledge, Logic, Logos, Memory, Mind, Sky, Speed, Wisdom
Qualities (negative)	Anxiety, Dispersion, Impulsiveness, Indecision, Insecurity, Nervousness, Paranoia, Prejudice, Theft

Fire - Works of Will

"When thou shalt behold that holy and formless Fire shining flashingly through the depths of the Universe: Hear thou the Voice of Fire." [11]

Axiom	To Will
Colour (Modern)	Red
Astrological Signs	Aries, Leo, Sagittarius
Planets	Mars, Sun
Direction	South or East
Time of Day	Noon
Season	Summer
Sense	Sight
Gender	Masculine
Tools	Dagger
Deities	Hades, Hephaistos
Tetragrammaton	Yod
Archangel	Michael
Demon King	Paimon
Enochian King	Edelperna
Enochian Divine Name	Oip Teaa Pedoce
Elemental Governor	Seruph (or Nathaniel)
Elemental King	Djin
Elementals	Salamanders
Kerub	Lion
Gem	Ruby
Metal	Gold, Iron
Tarot	Wands
Platonic Solid	Tetrahedron

---

11 Chaldean Oracles, No.199, C2nd CE.

The Greek philosopher Heraclitus suggested in the sixth century BCE that Fire was the universal cause, a view that would be echoed centuries later by some of the doctrines found in the *Chaldean Oracles of Zoroaster*.

Fire is an analytical masculine element, associated with the word (logos). In the macrocosm it is most obvious as the sun in the sky. Fire always causes transformation – it is neutral and contains the power to create or destroy. Thus in the *Perfect Sermon* (in the *Corpus Hermeticum*) Hermes says, *"Tis fire alone, in that it is borne upwards, giveth life; that which is carried downwards is subservient to fire."* In the *Old Testament* God is referred to three times as a *"consuming fire"*,[12] and the Bible is full of links between fire and divine and magickal events.

Fire is particularly associated with prayer, we are encouraged to *"enflame ourselves with prayer"* to achieve an ecstatic state where our passion fuels the intent and feeds it to the divine source it is offered to. The reference to the formless fire in the *Chaldean Oracles* is an example of this perception that fire is the holiest of the elements. Theodore Roszak captured the essence of this in his poem *Where the Wasteland Ends*, when he wrote:

> *"Unless the eye catch fire, the god will not be seen.*
> *Unless the ear catch fire, the god will not be heard.*
> *Unless the tongue catch fire, the god will not be named.*
> *Unless the heart catch fire, the god will not be loved.*
> *Unless the mind catch fire, the god will not be known."*[13]

Fire is the great transformer. Fire is the least obviously present around us on the Earth of the four elements, yet one expression of Fire

---

12 Deuteronomy 4:24 & 9:3, Hebrews 12:29.

13 Where the Wasteland Ends, Roszak, 1973.

is light, which enables us to see. It is the most subtle of the elements, it flickers and dances, leaping up to die down and be gone again. It is probably for this reason that it is sometimes referred to as the *'living element'*. The magickal axiom associated with fire is *To Will*, reflecting its creative, dynamic and energetic qualities. Through the light of fire we receive illumination, and can see our path, enabling the process of transformation that it facilitates to continue. Willpower is what keeps us on the path of achievement.

Fire is also associated with courage and freedom. To be free we must be brave, and be willing to use our creativity and drive to succeed. Fire motivates us to succeed and refine our passions. Fire can be creative or destructive, and this is clearly seen in nature. A forest fire may initially seem devastating, but many plants actually need fire in their life cycle to ensure their continued survival.

Fire burns, and reminds us of the importance of control. When handled properly fire provides light and heat, and can be used to cook and for protection. If allowed to get out of control it can cause great destruction. In the same way fire represents our will and our passions. If controlled they can be creative and constructive, enabling us to develop and do great things. But if we let them get out of control we can become obsessive, or violent.

Fire is probably the most challenging element, its creative and destructive power contained within every flame. Fire represents transformation, both in the substances which burn, and in the environment around it, as the flames supply light and heat. Fire burns with a passion and energy which are reflected in the human spirit. The purity of fire is like our motivation and will, the drive to succeed and shine with our own light. Fire gives us the energy to refine our passions and strive for our goals. Fire can leap up and die down again just as suddenly, and brings spontaneity in its flames. The dance of fire reminds us of our own dance of life.

An alchemical acronym for fire, or ignis, is *In Gehenna Nostræ Ignis Scientiæ*, meaning *"In Hell is the Fire of Our Science."* This emphasises the nature of subterranean fire, seen in views of the underworld such as the Greek Tartaros, the Hebrew Gehenna and the Christian Hell. From an alchemical perspective it emphasises the mystery of the fire in the earth, as the sun at midnight or black sun, thought to continue its daily journey through the underworld every night.

Working with the element of Fire enables you to concentrate on your drives and direction. Enhancing fiery qualities like courage, creativity, focus and motivation will help keep you fixed on the path, and using the drive, power and freedom of fire to fuel your will can only help keep you pure and motivated. Concentrating on the cathartic power of fire can help you burn away the negative emotional states that fire can bring as the destructive edge of its gifts. Transforming the cruelty, egotism, possessiveness and other destructive emotions in the crucible of your will in the flame of your spirit will help you to burn even brighter and with a truer essence.

Qualities (Positive)	Courage, Creativity, Drive, Energy, Focus, Freedom, Motivation, Passion, Power, Purity, Success, Transformation, Vision, Will
Qualities (Negative)	Anger, Cruelty, Egotism, Possessiveness, Vengeance, Violence

Water – Works of Daring

"Sublime waters ... which flow in their place, abundant waters which dwell together permanently in the great reservoir, children of the ocean which are seven, the waters are sublime, the waters are brilliantly pure, the waters glisten."[14]

Axiom	To Dare
Colour (Modern)	Blue
Astrological Signs	Cancer, Pisces, Scorpio
Planets	Jupiter*, Moon (Neptune)
Direction	West
Time of Day	Dusk
Season	Autumn
Sense	Taste
Gender	Feminine
Tools	Cup
Deities	Persephone (Nestis), Poseidon
Tetragrammaton	Heh
Archangel	Gabriel
Demon King	Ariton
Enochian King	Raagiosel
Enochian Divine Name	Empeh Arsel Gaiol
Elemental Governor	Tharsis
Elemental King	Niksa
Elementals	Undines
Kerub	Man
Gem	Sapphire
Metal	Mercury
Tarot	Cups
Platonic Solid	Icosahedron

---

14 Babylonian Hymn to the Waters, given in Chaldean Magic, Lenormant.

Of all the elements, Water is the one most often associated with the primal creation. The Sumerian creation myth has the divine couple of Apsu and Tiamat representing sweet water and salt water, the waters of the abyss. The Egyptian Ogdoad, of four primal divine couples, likewise focused on the *Nun* or primal waters. This idea of the primal waters as the foundation of creation is also found in the work of Thales of Miletius, the seventh century BCE philosopher who is considered the first of the Greek philosophers. Water is a feminine element, associated with matter (*hulê*). The thirteenth century Kabbalist Azriel of Gerona described water as the primeval mother who gave birth to darkness.

From a Kabbalistic perspective *'Living Water'* is water which has fallen as rain or is otherwise from a natural source such as a spring, and not been drawn from its source by an artificial conduit or by a human hand. This water has fallen straight from heaven, and is in a pure state. Living water is found in lakes, ponds, rivers and springs, and we may note the instructions in Grimoires like the *Key of Solomon* for the magician to bathe in a river or similar source of living water. It may also be used for purifying ritual items, and in talismanic magick. This is why dew is sometimes associated with the highest Sephira of Kether in Kabbalistic texts as living water.

Life began in the waters. Water is vital for life, and like fire it can be both nurturing and destructive. In the macrocosm Water is all around us as rain, rivers, lakes and oceans, covering much of our planet, and making up the bulk of our bodies. The seas move in tides, and this reflects our lives, which ebb and flow like those tides.

The dichotomy of water was expressed well by the Greek philosopher Heraclitus when he wrote, *"The sea is the purest and foulest water: for fish drinkable and life-sustaining; for men undrinkable and deadly."*[15] Likewise the pure water of a river or lake would be poisonous to sea creatures but sustains man and the other animals.

The magickal axiom of Water is *To Dare*, which we must do if we are to control our emotions and not let them run away with us, like a tidal wave. We must also dare to push the boundaries of our learning and our experience, another important step on any magickal path.

Water can represent both serenity, like the still surface of a lake, or sexual energy and love, which can be as changeable as the sea. Like Air, Water transports things, and this is reflected in the associated sense of taste, which tells us whether we like to eat or drink something. The dreamlike quality of Sun or Moon light sparkling on water also indicates another watery association, that of dreams. Our dreams are messages from the depths of our unconscious, rising to the surface of our consciousness like a whale from the depths.

Water can be nurturing, the *'waters of life'*, or it can symbolise death, the journey beyond the physical into the unknown, which has always been represented as a journey over water. The ancient Egyptian underworld, Amenti, was believed to be on the west of the river Nile, and the Celts saw the Isles of the Blessed (afterlife) as being in the west over the Atlantic Ocean. Such worldviews show that the link between water and the direction of the west has been symbolically present for thousands of years. Water additionally represents rebirth as well as death, and the compassion that comes from accepting inevitable change and encompassing it.

Water is unique amongst the four elements in that it can be solid (ice), liquid or gaseous (water vapour and steam). Its ability to change state reflects its quality of transformation, and adaptability to the appropriate condition. In Autumn we encounter the elemental tide of

---

15 Fragments, Heraclitus, C6th BCE.

water, in the rains that fall, and the sense of change that fills the air around us, as the tide of the year begins to ebb.

Water (aqua) is described by the alchemical acronym Aqua - *Album Quæ Vehit Aurum,* meaning *"Which Bears the White Gold."* The term white gold was used to describe liquid Mercury, also called the Water of the Philosophers.

Working with the element of Water helps you to concentrate on harmonising your emotional being. Water can help you to both enhance positive emotional states like compassion, serenity and nurturing, as well as transforming negative states like deceit, jealousy, spite and treachery. Water can also help you focus on your subtle senses, developing your empathy and psychism, and working with your dreams.

Qualities (Positive)	Compassion, Death, Dreams, Emotions, Empathy, Nurturing, Psychism, Serenity, Sexuality, Sympathy, Trust
Qualities (Negative)	Deceit, Fear, Hatred, Jealousy, Sorrow, Spite, Treachery

Earth – Works of Silence

*"Earth darkens all illuminative natures,
and produces shadow."*[16]

Axiom	To Keep Silent
Colour (Modern)	Green, Black
Astrological Signs	Capricorn, Taurus, Virgo
Planets	Saturn, Venus (Pluto)
Direction	North
Time of Day	Midnight
Season	Winter
Sense	Touch
Gender	Feminine
Tools	Pentacle
Deities	Hera, Gaia
Tetragrammaton	Heh (final)
Archangel	Uriel
Demon King	Amaimon
Enochian King	Izhikal
Enochian Divine Name	Emor Dial Hectega
Elemental Governor	Ariel
Elemental King	Ghob
Elementals	Gnomes
Kerub	Bull
Gem	Emerald
Metal	Lead, Copper
Tarot	Disks
Platonic Solid	Cube

---

16 Fragments, Proclus, C5th CE.

Earth is a feminine element associated with matter (*hulê*). In the macrocosm it is most obvious as the ground beneath our feet, giving us the solidity of physicality and form. With form come qualities like endurance, patience, tolerance and steadfastness. Earth is further associated with sensuality and the sense of touch.

The magickal axiom of earth is *To Be Silent*. This describes the enduring stillness of earth, which can be felt when standing alone on a mountain or in a field, and which is reflected in the inner silence of meditation and contemplation. The silence of Earth also reflects its non-judgmental nature, which by its very selflessness encourages us to be the same, to be responsible in our actions, to try and make our world something of beauty, and leave it better than we found it. The silence of a winter's day, when the world is blanketed with snow, when even water has been given the solidity of earth as ice and snow, emphasises the elemental tide of earth at its peak.

Earth is a nurturing element, providing the food we eat, and making up the materials used to build houses, and indeed being the ground beneath our feet. Earth teaches us that through dedication, patience and toil, all things are possible. Earth is nature as well as nurture, and all we do impacts on the people we are and the environment we live in. Earth is the element that is most often taken for granted, yet it is our home, supplying all our needs.

As the giver of form, earth also represents manifestation. Manifestation can represent several levels of activity. On a physical level it can be the manifestation of a conclusion or result, the end goal of a process. On an emotional level it can be the realisation of a desire or dream. The same is true on a magickal level, or it can be the physical appearance of a spiritual creature in a tangible form.

The practicality of earth is emphasised in the importance of being grounded, one which is frequently absent or ignored by people who get wrapped up in the glamour of magick, and forget that at the end of the day, earth provides the test of solidity. An alchemical acronym for earth, or Terra is *Trium Elementorum Receptaculum Recondo Aurifodinam*, meaning *"I Conceal the Gold bearing Refuge of Three Elements."* This emphasises the form-giving qualities of earth as the source not only of gold (and by implication the other metals and minerals) but also the solidified forms of the other elements such as ice and lava. In the *Corpus Hermeticum*, Hermes says of earth, *"Tis earth alone, in that it resteth on itself, that is the Receiver of all things, and also the Restorer of all genera that it receives."*[17]

Working with the element of Earth helps you develop both the physical and emotional-social side of your being. On the physical side you can enhance qualities such as endurance, practicality and strength. On the emotional and social side, patience, tolerance, selflessness, humility and pragmatism can all help you not waste energy and actually benefit from your social life and emotional interactions.

The negative earthy qualities are ones which need to be transformed whenever they appear, and they tend to recur like deep-rooted weeds, you cannot just bury them and hope they will go away. Vigilance will help you spot the signs of negative Earth behaviour, which you can then transform into positive Earth contributing to your progress forwards.

Qualities (Positive)	Endurance, Humility, Patience, Practicality, Pragmatism, Realism, Responsibility, Selflessness, Sensuality, Stability, Stillness, Strength, Tolerance
Qualities (Negative)	Attention-seeking, Depression, Domineering, Greed, Inertia, Laziness, Melancholy, Stubbornness

---

17 The Perfect Sermon, Thrice-Greatest Hermes, Mead (ed).

CHAPTER 3

Elemental Interaction

"Elements, each other greeting,
Gifts and powers attend your meeting!"[18]

As physical and spiritual realities, the four elements are around us at all times, and they are constantly interacting. The method of their interaction is one of transformation or domination. The principles for this interaction were originally laid out by the Greek philosopher Aristotle, and then subsequently developed many centuries later by the Spanish mystic Raymon Lull (1229-1315 CE).

The interaction depends on the quantities of the elements and also whether they share qualities or not. Elements which do not share common qualities can also not be transformed into each other. They can only be dominated or overcome by the element which is present in a greater quantity. In an equal quantity they effectively neutralise each other. Thus the polarities of fire and water, and of earth and air, cannot be transformed into each other. In the right circumstances the conjunction of opposites may lead to a greater whole, and this is one of the fundamental principles of physical alchemy.

---

18 The Pirate, Scott, 1833.

When two elements with a common quality interact, the element which is present in a greater quantity will overcome the lesser quantity element. For example air and water are both moist, but if a greater quantity of air acts on a smaller quantity of water, the warmth of the air would overcome the coolness of the water, i.e. it would evaporate. This process is reversible - if the air containing a smaller quantity of water came into contact with a greater quantity of water, the water held in the air would become water again, i.e. it would precipitate (rain) or condense.

Aristotle observed that when two opposing elements are acted upon by a third element, the third element can draw a quality from each of the two opposing elements and transform them into itself. Thus earth and air are in opposition, but if e.g. they were acted upon by fire, the fire would draw the warmth from air and the dryness from the earth and transform them into itself.

Effectively we can see that the earth would provide the physical fuel and the air would provide the correct sustenance (oxygen) to enable the fire to grow.

Raymon Lull observed that if elements which share a quality combine in equal measure the element in which that quality is dominant will overcome the other element. Thus fire will overcome air, air will overcome water, water will overcome earth, and earth will overcome fire. In each instance the more subtle element overcomes the less subtle element, with the exception of earth, which overcomes fire.

A theory which had developed by the Renaissance was that the fifth element existed where the other four elements were in balance. The fifth element, now commonly known as Spirit, is also sometimes referred to as Aether, or Quintessence (literally *'fifth essence'*). Plato posited its existence in his work *Timaeus*, and Aristotle included it in his cosmology of the elements. Subsequent philosophers would amend the views of the Quintessence, so that Plotinus in the third century CE considered it intangible and penetrative, whilst Philostratus described it as the air breathed by the gods.

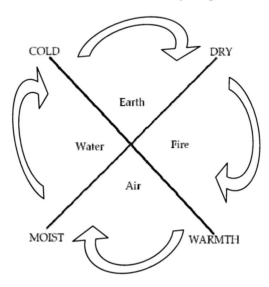

By the Renaissance this was alluded to by Robert Fludd in his *Mosaical Philosophy* as being *'subtler than light'*. In the key alchemical text known as the Emerald Tablet, Aether's relationship to the four elements is described allegorically:

> *"The father thereof is the Sun [fire],*
> *The mother the Moon [water].*
> *The wind [air] carried it in its womb,*
> *The earth [earth] is the nurse thereof.*
> *It is the father of all works of wonder*
> *throughout the whole world.*
> *The power thereof is perfect."*

Aether is frequently equated with the life-force, or more specifically with the soul or sentience, these being often equated with each other as it is believed by many that if something has sentience it must also have a soul. This may be extended even further, to the notion that Aether represents the impartial divine essence of life seeking to evolve whilst permeating the universe. This is not a new idea, as may be seen from Philostratus' work *The Life of Apollonius of Tyana*, where Apollonius asks if the universe is a living creature, and he receives the response, *"Yes if you have a sound knowledge of it, for it engenders all living things."*

Perhaps a good way to describe Aether would be as the intangible expression of life manifesting with intent. To further clarify and express this term we will resort to the ancient wisdom of the *Tao Teh King*, which in defining the Tao gives us a wonderful description of Aether:

"Look, it cannot be seen – it is beyond form.
Listen, it cannot be heard – it is beyond sound.
Grasp, it cannot be held – it is intangible...
From above it is not bright;
From below it is not dark: ← GOD
An unbroken thread beyond description.
It returns to nothingness.
The form of the formless,
The image of the imageless,
It is called indefinable and beyond imagination.
Stand before it and there is no beginning.
Follow it and there is no end."[19]

---

19 Tao Teh King, verse 14.

Elemental Body Meditation

In this meditation you will explore the four elements, their presence, effects and interaction within your body. Start by preparing yourself as you usually do for meditation. When you are comfortable you can begin, focusing on each element in turn starting with Air.

Meditation:

Concentrate on the breath entering and leaving your body. Feel the air as it passes through your nostrils and/or mouth and down your throat into your lungs. Focus on how the air is transported all around your body in your blood, with the oxygen you have inhaled being transported to your tissues and the waste carbon dioxide being transported back to your lungs to be exhaled with surplus water. Be aware of the spaces in your body occupied by air, such as in your mouth, your ears, your lungs, and realise that air is present throughout your body.

Next concentrate on how the element of fire is present within yourself. Feel the fire of digestion in your stomach, as food is turned into fuel for the body. Feel the fire of electricity as messages are sent along your nerves, synapses sparking and passing on all the signals that keep your body functioning, that represent your thoughts as the connections are made in your brain. Consider how your eyes receive light and convert it into the images they send to your brain, from light to electricity to perception.

Now move on to the element of water within your body. Think of the water in your saliva, in your eyes, the subtle moisture within you. Then consider all the water in your blood and other fluids that flow around your body transporting all the different types of fuel, hormones, antibodies, and everything your body needs to function. Be aware of how water that makes up the bulk of the tissues in your body, and also runs along your veins and arteries like a giant system of rivers.

Finally consider the element of earth within you, the solidity of your bones that makes your skeleton and teeth that enable you to chew food. Think of the earthy substances that cover you, your nails, your hair and your skin. Appreciate how the muscles and fat in your body are the strength and endurance of the element of earth. Consider how earth gives you form and defines the shape you are.

When you have finished considering the element of earth, appreciate how all the elements work in harmony to create the temple of your body. Through their balance you exist, and your body is the temple of aether, your soul and vitality, your mind and intent and emotions. Allow this understanding to sink in, and then open your eyes.

Do this EVERY Day you can!

and don't judge yourself if you don't do it for what you think is an unacceptable amount of time

CHAPTER 4

Exploring the Elements

The meditations given in this chapter will help you to explore each element in turn. They should be repeated over a period of time in order to cultivate a depth of knowledge and understanding through experience. For each in turn prepare yourself as you would ordinarily do for meditation, making sure to have prepared the items you will require.

Air Meditation

For the air meditation you need a censer with charcoal and some incense. A pure resin like frankincense or myrrh is preferable as it retains a consistent smell as it burns. If you are meditating indoors it is preferable to have some ventilation so there is a flow of air through the room.

Light the charcoal and when it is glowing hot, put some resin on to it. Watch the smoke start to curl up into the room, and smell its fragrance as it fills the room. See how the smoke gives form and colour to the air, though this is transient as it dissipates, changing shape and fading into invisibility, leaving its fragrance as evidence for its passing.

As the smoke shifts, consider how air is always in motion, the winds that blow, whether they be as fierce gales or gentle breezes. Even when it seems completely still, there is still movement of air going on in the sky, or over the surface of bodies of water. Reflect on how movement is a quality of air, it transports sound enabling communication, its intangible gaseous structure is also the perfect medium for light to travel through. Air moves or permits movement in the physical world. Air represents the powers of the intellect and knowledge, again showing how it is associated with movement, of ideas and perceptions. (When the incense has stopped smoking add some more.)

The subtlety of air mirrors the immeasurability of life. You know things are alive, but the spark of life in them is present throughout them and is somehow elusive, just as air engenders life through its content, being the breath of life, and yet is also elusive. Contemplate the subtlety of air and appreciate how all its qualities are tied in with this and its quality of movement.

Flame Meditation

For the flame meditation all you require is a candle and a dark room. For best results the candle should be a beeswax taper. Failing that a white wax taper is preferable. Place the candle on a table about three foot (1m) from the wall (which should be blank). Ensure the curtains are closed and that there is no other light in the room, not even the stand-by light of an electrical device. Light the candle and give it a minute to take. Then sit comfortably in a chair by the table, ideally so that you are about three foot from the candle.

As you see the dancing flames, leaping with the joy of pure energy, gaze deep into the flames and see the blue inner flames that represent the flame of spirit, the energy that fills your soul and empowers your magick. If you look deep within the blueness you may see shades of white, where the very essence of the flame reveals itself in sparks and flashes, hinting at gateways to beyond

Now move your attention to the outer parts of the flames, burning yellow, representing the material essence of the flame, where the inner fire is fed by the air and transforms itself and the air through its action. Orange and red tints show the collision of the physical and the astral, as the flame devours all within its environment.

Now look between the outer edges of the flames and the light emanating from the flames. In that liminal space you may perceive a sky blue-blackness, like the night sky. This is the shadow of the stars, where the starfire of above is reflected in the earthfire down below. Draw that power from the flame, the power of the starfire, in the light that shines on to you, feel it being absorbed into your body, empowering your psychic senses, awakening the latent power in you as you grow stronger

Living Water Meditation

'Living Water' (*mayim hayim*) is water which has fallen from the sky bringing the purity of heaven with it, and has not been drawn from its source by pipes or a human hand. Living water is found in lakes, ponds, rivers and springs, and may be collected as dew by leaving a bowl out overnight during the appropriate seasons. By the definition this is not something that would really fit with acid rain in a big city, which would not perhaps be living water in the same way as was originally meant. However if you can go and visit a suitable site in the countryside and collect water from a spring or overnight dew, you can use it for magickal work and meditation. To gather water not

by hand, put a bowl in the water so it is filled by the water, and then extricate it, so it has not strictly speaking been gathered by a human hand. If you do go to a spring, then that is a preferable site for the following meditation, rather than at home.

Sit next to the water (be it a pool, spring, bowl, etc) and watch the surface of the water. Consider how this water is living water, which has been transformed into vapour, and possibly also into ice. It has experienced many changes of state, and will experience more, for water is a medium of transformation, going through change and also creating change.

Place your face as close as you conveniently (and safely) can to the water and say your magickal name over the surface of the water. (This is an old Qabalistic practice, of only speaking words of power over water, probably based on *Genesis 1:2*). Watch the surface of the water to see if it is moved by your breath, and see the small ripples spread, showing how a simple act can have repercussions which continue for a long time afterwards.

As you gaze at the water, you feel its still, mirror-like surface calm you, and you recall how the practice of hydromancy, or water divination, was used in ancient times to see spiritual creatures and other places. As you look at the living water, you start to be aware that it is also a gateway of possibility. Allow yourself to see any visions which may unfold, but if they do not, be aware that some of the living water is evaporating and surrounding you as you gaze. Dip a fingertip into the water and anoint your brow with the water. Repeat this for your eyelids, and then drop a drop of the water into your mouth. Be aware of the power contained within even the smallest drop of water, and how it can be used to purify and also open doorways for you.

Silent Earth Meditation

This meditation may be performed anywhere that you will have privacy where you can stand with your bare feet on earth beneath you. The ideal would be a wood or hill, but anywhere you will not be disturbed and can make the connection between your feet and the earth below is fine.

Take off your shoes and socks and feel the earth beneath your feet. Feel the texture and temperature, is it cool to the touch or warm? Feel the sense of silent strength and immense power that rises up from the earth beneath you into your feet. Be aware of the stillness that you are connecting to, and which is surrounding you like a cocoon. Notice how your thought patterns change and slow, and the silence manifests through an inner silence which leaves you hearing the sounds of your body. You become aware of the blood flowing through your veins, and the breath in your lungs.

As time passes even the sounds of your body fade away and you feel the silence within you, the immense and ancient silence of the earth, the awesome might which quickens life and encourages growth. You become aware of your connection to this web of life, and feel its strength within you. With this the connection fades and your awareness returns to your body and your surroundings.

CHAPTER 5

The Unification Rite

"Apollonius again asked which was the first of the elements, and Iarchas answered: 'All are simultaneous, for a living creature is not born bit by bit.'" [20]

The practice of the Unification Rite which follows is entirely centred on the magickal axiom of *'As above, so below.'* This is arguably the most significant of all magickal doctrines, from its roots in the Sumerian Inanna myths[21] to the alchemy of the Emerald Tablet and in the Qabalah. The axiom of *As above, so below* sums up the whole principle of sympathetic (or contagious) magick. It states that our actions are both influenced by the universe and also influence the universe. Normally the matter of scale dictates that the above, the universe or macrocosm, has a greater influence on the below, the person or microcosm. However if you are the fulcrum at the right place and at the right time, who is to say what can or cannot be achieved? Consider pivotal moments in history and you will appreciate that sometimes a single simple act may have repercussions throughout the world and beyond.

---

20 The Life of Apollonius of Tyana, Philostratus, 220 CE.

21 From the Great Above to the Great Below.

For any act of magick you should be in a state of balance. This has implications, for to be balanced you have to conduct yourself in certain ways, adopt a suitable lifestyle, train yourself to harness your abilities, the list goes on. So whilst it is true that magick can be extremely simple, perhaps it is also true to say that to prepare yourself to perform effective magick, whilst also simple, is a disciplined process which cannot effectively be undertaken on a whim. What might seem like simple temple skills can take many years to perfect.

The *As above, so below* formula permeates the Western Esoteric Traditions. It contains within it many layers of meaning, but most of all it is an allegory for the interconnectedness of all things. The Orphic Oath emphasises the presence of this key axiom in the mystery traditions – the declaration that *"I am a child of earth and starry heaven"* is a proclamation to the universe of realisation of the universal nature of the individual. This then is essentially the process of the Great Work, being the focal point of your own existence and directing your intent towards perfection. Then truly you are living *As above, so below*.

If you have not worked with this formula before you should take some time to contemplate it prior to undertaking the Unification Rite of the Four Elements as a personal understanding of its importance will help intensify the ritual experience for you.

The Unification Rite of the Four Elements

This rite is a ceremonial balancing of the elements within yourself for use prior to or as part of a ritual.

You will need:

- Censer of incense
- Candle (preferably red)
- Chalice of water
- Pentacle

Take the censer of incense from the altar and walk to the east. Hold the censer of incense up to the east, and visualise the triangle of Air in vibrant yellow behind the censer, saying:

Air be thou adored within and without, as above, so below

Breathe the incense smoke in, feeling the power of air within yourself as the fragrance of the incense permeates the room. Circumambulate the rest of the circle clockwise back to the east holding the censer and return it to the altar.

Take the candle from the altar and walk to the south. Hold the candle up to the south, and visualise the red triangle of Fire behind the candle, saying:

Fire be thou adored within and without, as above, so below

Watch the dancing flame, and wait for it to move towards you, showing the connection between you and fire; feel the power of fire within yourself, the flame of your will. Circumambulate the rest of the circle clockwise back to the south holding the candle and return it to the altar.

Take the chalice of water from the altar and walk to the west. Hold the chalice of water up to the west, and visualise the downward pointing blue triangle of Water behind the chalice, saying:

Water be thou adored within and without, as above, so below

Bring the chalice to your lips and taste a sip of the water, feeling the power of water flowing into you and through you as the water flows down your throat. Circumambulate the rest of the circle clockwise back to the west holding the chalice and return to the altar.

Take the pentacle from the altar and walk to the north. Hold the pentacle up to the north, visualise the earth triangle in a verdant green behind the pentacle and say:

Earth be thou adored within and without, as above, so below

Hold the pentacle to your chest so it is in front of your heart, and feel the connection between the power of earth and the physicality of your form; feel your own physical power. Circumambulate the rest of the circle clockwise back to the north holding the pentacle and return it to the altar.

CHAPTER 6

The Elemental Archangels

"Michael, Gabriel, Raphael, Uriel, the holy angels who stand before him who dwells in the heavens, the holy and exalted one."[22]

Although it may seem confusing, the archangels attributed to the elements are also planetary archangels. However their associations do effectively demonstrate the elemental attributions of some of the planets by association. Thus the solar Michael is the archangel of Fire, the lunar Gabriel is the archangel of Water, the Mercurial Raphael is the archangel of Air, and the Venusian Uriel is the archangel of Earth. The archangels are not beings of the elemental realms, rather they act in the role of overseer of the realm, standing outside and controlling all within.

As well as being the four archangels who stand before God, these archangels are also the same four who are invoked to protect a person whilst they sleep in the Jewish protective ritual of *Kriat Shema al ha-Mitah*. The prayer for protection clearly influenced the creation of the Lesser Banishing Ritual of the Pentagram by the Golden Dawn, and is as follows:

---

22 Leiden, Anastasi No.9; Ancient Christian Magic; Meyer; 1999.

In the name of Adonai the God of Israel:
May the angel Michael be at my right,
And the angel Gabriel be at my left;
And in front of me the angel Uriel;
And behind me the angel Raphael;
And above my head the Shekinah.

The significance of these four archangels of the elements may also be seen by the fact that they are the only four archangels found in Islam, albeit with an alternative name in the case of Uriel (Azrael), or Arabic versions of the names for Gabriel (Jibrail) and Raphael (Israfel). Only Michael and Gabriel are named in the Bible, though Raphael is in the *Book of Tobit*, and he and Uriel both appear in the *Book of Enoch*.

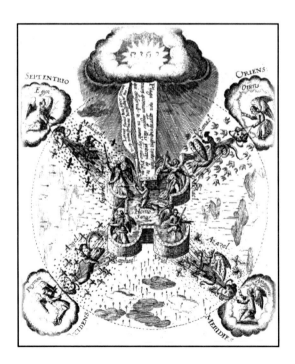

These four archangels are from the order of angels called the Seraphim, or 'Fiery Ones', who are considered to be made of Fire. Many of the main archangels, specifically the seven who are in the presence of God, (and including some of those that fell like Lucifer), come from this order. They are referred to in Psalms when it says, *"Who maketh his angels winds; his ministers a flaming fire."*[23]

Angel	Raphael	Michael	Gabriel	Uriel
Face	Slender, Ethereal, Androgynous	Stern, Beautiful, Masculine	Blindingly Beautiful, Feminine	Strong, Feminine, Beautiful
Eyes	Sky Blue	Golden-Red	Violet-Blue	Green
Hair	Blonde	Red-Brown	Silvery	Black
Robe	Yellow	Scarlet	Blue	Green
Tools	Caduceus Pilgrim's Staff Alabaster Jar	Flaming Sword Lance Golden Scales	Silver Cup Lily topped Staff	Copper Lamp Flame Sword

---

23 Psalms 104:4.

The Archangel of Air - Raphael

Raphael means *"Healer of God"*, and he is the archangel charged with healing mankind and the earth. He is the Archangel of the element of Air, and patron of travellers, often being depicted with a pilgrim's staff, and he protects those on journeys, especially air travel.

As well as protecting travellers, Raphael's special charges are the young and innocent, as can be seen from the story of him protecting the boy Tobiah from a demon (*Tobit 3-6*).

Raphael is the archangel of knowledge and communication, and may be called to help with any related areas, such as improving your memory, learning languages, exams, dealing with bureaucracy and business matters. He was said to have healed the earth after the Flood, and also visited Noah after the Flood to give him a book of medicine, which had belonged to the archangel Raziel.

Raphael is usually portrayed with a beautiful slender androgynous face. He may bear a caduceus in his right hand, or occasionally a white alabaster jar of healing herbs or ointment.

Contemplation on Raphael

Visualise Raphael standing on top of a wind-swept hill, with white heather carpeting the grass at his feet. He is around 3m tall, and wears a yellow robe with brown leather sandals. Flashes of purple appear around his form as he moves.

His face is slender and ethereal, with an androgynous quality, framed with yellow blonde hair and containing piercing sky blue eyes that seem to see forever.

On his back are a large pair of white wings. Raphael bears a caduceus in his right hand and a white alabaster jar in his left hand. You realise he is present in his role of divine healer, and as you consider this you feel a flow of air around you, like a gentle breeze blowing past Raphael and into your space, whispering to you as it enters.

The Archangel of Fire - Michael

Michael was the first angel created, and is often seen as the leader of the angels or *"first among equals"*. His name means *"He who is like God"*. He is usually shown wielding a sword or lance, and sometimes the scales of justice. As the archangel of the element of Fire and the Sun, he helps those who call him to achieve goals and destinies. He is particularly associated with protection, marriage and music. Michael is the defender of the just and is also known as the Merciful Angel. Michael has been particularly popular for inclusion in protective amulets, and significantly his name is included in the triangle of evocation used in Grimoires like the *Lemegeton*.[24] Michael was the angel described in the third century CE text, *The Testament of Solomon* as giving King Solomon the ring inscribed with the pentagram that enabled him to bind demons, and force them to build his temple.

Michael appears a number of times in the Bible in a manner symbolically appropriate to his nature. Thus Michael was the archangel who appeared to Moses as the fire in the burning bush (*Exodus 2:5*), he rescued Abraham from the fiery furnace of Nimrod (*Genesis Rabbah 44:13*) and he also rescued Daniel from the lion's den (*Daniel 6:22*; note the lion as a symbol of fire). Michael appears in *Revelations* as the leader of the celestial host that defeats the antichrist, and he is the prayer-leader in the Heavens in Islam.

---

24 See The Goetia of Dr Rudd, Skinner & Rankine, 2007.

Contemplation on Michael

Visualise Michael standing on the edge of a volcano. He is around 3m tall, and wears a scarlet robe with brown leather sandals. Flashes of green appear around his form as he moves. His face is stern and beautiful, with a masculine quality, framed with red-brown hair and fiery golden-red eyes that seem to burn with an inner light. On his back are a large pair of white wings. Michael bears a flaming sword in his right hand and a set of golden scales in his left hand. You realise he is present in his role of divine warrior, and as you consider this you feel a blast of dry heat blow into your space, bringing a feeling of power with it.

The Archangel of Water - Gabriel

Gabriel means *'The Strength of God'*, and he is one of the fiery Seraphim. Gabriel is the angel who usually delivers messages to humanity, embodying the link between man and the universe and the divine as expressed by the Moon.

Gabriel first appears in the Old Testament in the book of *Daniel*. It was Gabriel who first indicated the coming of a messiah to Daniel in this book. Gabriel visited Zachary to tell him his son would be called John (the Baptist) and most famously he told Mary that she was pregnant with Jesus. In Islam Gabriel is also seen as the divine messenger, it was he who delivered the *Qur'an* to Mohammed.

As the Archangel of the Moon and the element of Water, Gabriel is the guide to the inner tides of our unconscious. Gabriel can help with developing the imagination and psychic abilities. He is also associated with domestic matters, especially the development of the home, or finding a new home. Gabriel can appear as male or female, and may be called to as either.

Contemplation on Gabriel

Visualise Gabriel standing by a waterfall with white lilies by his feet. He is around 3m tall, and wears a blue robe with brown leather sandals. Flashes of orange appear around his form as he moves. His face is blindingly beautiful, with a feminine quality, framed with silvery hair and violet-blue eyes that seem to brim with wisdom and knowledge. On his back are a large pair of white wings.

Gabriel bears a simple silver chalice in his right hand and a staff topped with lilies in his left hand. You realise he is present in his role of divine messenger, and as you realise this you feel cool moisture entering your space, bringing a feeling of knowledge and answers to half-forgotten questions with it.

The Archangel of Earth - Uriel

Uriel, also known as Auriel or Oriel, is the Archangel of the element of Earth, and of peace and salvation. His name means *"Light of God"*, and he is often depicted with a flame or lamp in his hands. Uriel is particularly associated with magickal power, and the application of force (an extreme example being his patronage of earthquakes). As such he is the angel to help cause a positive breaking of bonds when needed and overcoming inertia. He is also the patron of astrology and has been linked strongly with electricity.

Uriel is credited with being the angel who gave alchemy and the Qabalah to man. Uriel was the angel who helped inspire Abraham to lead the Jews out of Ur. As one of the most powerful archangels, Uriel is said to be the bearer of the keys to hell, standing as guardian to that infernal realm. He usually carries a copper lamp or flame in his hand.

Contemplation on Uriel

Visualise Uriel standing by the edge of a corn field with a wood behind him. He is around 3m tall, and wears a green robe with brown leather sandals. Flashes of red appear around his form as he moves. His face is beautiful and full of strength, with a feminine quality. It is framed with black hair and has green eyes that seem to shine with the light of understanding and hope. On his back are a large pair of white wings.

Uriel bears a copper lamp in his right hand which gives off a soft illumination, and a sword in his left hand. You realise he is present in his role of breaker of bonds, and as you realise this you feel a sense of strength and freedom entering your space, bringing a feeling of liberation and power with it.

CHAPTER 7

The Elemental Beings

"The Nymphs of the Fountains, and all the Water Spirits,
and terrestrial, aerial and astral forms, are the Lunar Riders and Rulers of all
Matter, the Celestial, the Starry, and that which lies in the Abysses."[25]

The Elemental beings are powerful and primal, they are the pure essence of the physical forms of matter in its diversity. As such they should be treated with respect, although you should also bear in mind that elemental beings vary in their type, and many are single-minded creatures embodying the power of their element. This single-mindedness is both their strength and weakness, for it can provide huge amounts of energy, but it tends to be inflexible.

However although they were not called elementals or *saganae* (meaning *'elements'*) until the works of Paracelsus in the Middle Ages, we can see that the same beings were previously described in the ancient world. Iamblichus in his classic fourth century CE work *Theurgia* discussed daimons (spirits), and introduced the idea that they could be elemental in nature, and did not maintain a physical corporality in the same way as man.

This concept was developed by Proclus in the fifth century CE, who divided the daimons (spirits) into five classes of being, rulers of

---

25 Chaldean Oracles, No.103.

Fire, Air, Water, Earth and the Underworld, thus providing an elemental division by kingdom which would evolve into the worldview espoused by Paracelsus.

The medieval view of elementals expressed by Paracelsus in his classic work *Liber de nymphis, sylphis, pygmaeis et salamandris et de caeteris spiritibus* was that they often appeared in human form, and frequently lived among men.

A reason for this was that they did not have a soul, and if they married a human they gained a soul, and likewise any offspring with a human would automatically have a soul. This was discussed in another major work regarding elementals, the *'fictional' Le Comte de Gabalis* by Monfaucon De Villars (1670), which was heavily plagiarised by Giuseppe Francesco Borri in his *La Chiave Del Gabinetto* (1681). These books were describing elemental beings who could appear in human form, which should not automatically be equated to the term elemental, which is normally used for the simplest forms of elemental creatures, and is a term we prefer not to use, to avoid confusion. Other writers would support Paracelsus, often quoting his work wholesale or paraphrased, as in this case from Thomas Rudd in the seventeenth century, when he wrote:

"Iamblichus saith, they are not men, because they walk spiritually; they cannot be spirits, because they eat, drink and have flesh and blood; they are therefore a peculiar Creature, and from their double nature they are made one mixture as any compounded matter of sweet and sour, or like two colours under one species."[26]

The desire for a soul suggested by Paracelsus is an interesting idea, as it goes some way to explaining the willingness of elemental

---

26 Harley MSS 6482, C17th CE.

creatures to respond to the call for aid from a magician. For surely they would not come and assist if they did not get something from the interaction? So perhaps as is suggested by De Villars, repeated exposure to magickal work may also go some way towards assisting the evolution of elemental beings, for it would be arrogant to assume that only we as humans are striving to evolve further.

The argument is that in gaining a soul an elemental creature gains immortality, immeasurably extending its long life span. Medieval texts suggested that a humanoid elemental creature had a lifespan of several hundred years, as described in the sixteenth century *De Subtilate Rerum* of Hieronymus Cardanus:

> *"On August 12, 1492, at two o'clock in the afternoon,*
> *there appeared to my father, when he had just said his prayers,*
> *seven men in silk garments in the Greek style.*
> *They wore purple half-boots and shining carmine red shirts.*
> *Their stature was unusually large. The heads of the spirits were uncovered*
> *and they looked to be approaching the age of forty although they themselves*
> *affirmed that they were over two hundred years old.*
> *When asked who they were, they replied that they were air spirits which arose*
> *in the air and dissolved into it once again, though they were able to prolong*
> *their lives to three hundred years."*[27]

Over the years we noticed that there does not seem to be any extant conjurations for the elementals in magickal texts spanning many centuries. This point is also made in the book *A Rosicrucian Notebook*:

> *"And we need hardly wonder at the scarcity of genuine Rosicrucian writings*
> *on the transmutation of metals when, generally speaking, no instructions*
> *have come down to us for summoning the elemental spirits."*[28]

---

27 De Subtilitate Rarum, Book IX, Cardanus, 1550.

In fact the examples of working with elementals given in books are in works of fiction, such as *Le Comte de Gabalis* (1670) and *The Pirate* (1821) by Sir Walter Scott.

The prayers of the elementals given by Eliphas Levi in his work *Transcendental Magic* are not actually directed toward the elementals, but rather they are from the elementals to God. These take their form from the prayer of the salamanders in *Le Comte de Gabalis* by de Villars, of which Levi's prayer of the salamanders is a paraphrased copy.

Having discussed elementals in a general sense, we will conclude this section with a quote from *Faust* which unites the different types in a charm.

> *"Salamanders, burn and glow;*
> *Water-spirits, twine and flow;*
> *Up, ye sylphs, in æther blue;*
> *Earthly goblins, down with you.*
> *He who could not win consent*
> *From each subject element,*
> *Could not govern at his will*
> *Spirits, be they good or ill.*
> *Salamanders, mix in flame;*
> *In your waters, sprites, the same;*
> *Sylphs, shine out in meteor beauty;*
> *Goblins, help to do your duty.*
> *Incubus, Incubus,*
> *Make the spell complete for us."*[29]

---

28 A Rosicrucian Notebook, Schrödter, 1992.

29 Faust, Goethe, 1824 translation by Galt.

The Elemental Rulers

The first reference to a group of elemental rulers is found in *Liber Juratus* in the thirteenth century, where they are called elemental angels or dominators. These are Cherub (air), Seraph or Nathaniel (fire), Tharsis (water) and Ariel (earth). The same four beings are subsequently referred to by Agrippa in his *Three Books of Occult Philosophy*, as well as in *The Magical Calendar* and in the *Semiphoras and Shemhamphorash of King Solomon* in the same role. In the *Key of Solomon* the four names are used in one of the Jupiterian pentacles, for protection from all earthly perils. Significantly they are set in an equal-armed cross in a circle, in the symbol of planet Earth, with a verse from *Psalm 22:16-17* around the edge. We use these names as part of the elemental pentacle design to good effect, as will be seen subsequently.

The names may seem somewhat confusing, as Cherub is also the name of a type of angel, and Ariel has several attributions, though these do include the appropriate rulership of the triplicity of zodiacal Earth signs. However the use of confusing names is also seen with those promoted by Eliphas Levi in his books for the elemental kings, which have moved into popular usage. These are Paralda (air), Djin (fire), Nicsa or Niksa (water) and Ghob (earth).

The name Djin is clearly drawn from the Arabic Djinn, the fire spirits popularised in the West as the genie. Niksa derives from nixie, the treacherous German shapeshifting water spirit found in folklore. The king of the Gnomes was called Gob in medieval tales, hence the name Ghob for the king of the Earth elementals. The name Paralda however does not seem to have any precedent in earlier mythology or folklore.

The different names for the elemental rulers does not indicate a separate set of beings, rather they are groups of names for the same beings. This is significant, as through the centuries different magicians and groups have found names through experience which work for them. Whether you prefer the names from *Liber Juratus*, or the names given by Levi, or another set of names which work for you is a matter of personal preference and experience.

What is important with the elemental rulers is their role as directors of the energy of their elements. An elemental ruler is hugely powerful compared to a simple elemental being. The lowest level Elemental beings are simple creatures, with a specific purpose and little intelligence. The elemental rulers are usually visualised in human or semi-human form, recalling the words of Friederich Fouqué in his novel *Undine* (1811):

> *"You must know, my sweet one, that there are beings in the elements which look almost like you (children of men) but do not let you glimpse them very often."* [30]

Element	Archangel	Ruler (Liber Juratus)	Ruler (Levi)
Air	Raphael	Cherub	Paralda
Fire	Michael	Seraph	Djin
Water	Gabriel	Tharsis	Niksa
Earth	Uriel	Ariel	Ghob

---

30 Undine, Fouqué, 1811.

Classification of Elemental Beings

During our elemental work over the years, we have developed a system of classification to make it easier to facilitate the choice of appropriate elemental creatures for magickal work. Although traditionally there are no descriptions of hierarchies of elemental beings, the idea is implied in the works of Paracelsus and subsequent writers. Paracelsus described the elemental realms having their own rulers, hierarchies and courts, indicating a clear power structure. Taking the angelic hierarchies as the best model of a hierarchy of spiritual creatures, we applied the same principles to establishing hierarchies for the creatures of each of the four elemental realms.

The categories we put in place enable the magician to choose the appropriate beings to work with, and also which to avoid. At the top of the hierarchy is the one type of creature which is not actually part of the realm, the archangel who oversees the elemental realm. The subsequent levels of the hierarchy do not form an absolute hard and fast system, it is included to show the types of elemental being in each realm, and their relative levels of power and complexity.

We have avoided using the term elemental as a stand-alone term, as we feel it has led to a great deal of confusion. Instead we use the term elemental being, which covers a range of different creatures. This then avoids the situation of different types of beings all being lumped together inappropriately under the same term, such as salamander. For e.g. the term, Vulcan or Aetnean is used to describe a humanoid fire being, whereas a salamander is usually perceived as having a lizard form (though the creatures are amphibians).

Categories of Elemental Beings

Level	Creature	Notes
Overseer	Archangel	Not an elemental creature in the accepted manner, rather an extremely powerful and evolved director of energies
Ruler	Ruler	Extremely powerful and complex entity who governs the element
Aristocracy	Shapeshifter	Intelligent and powerful amoral elemental being with the ability to assume different forms
Genius	Guardian	An elemental which has become tied to a specific location and assumed the role of guardian spirit, often (but not always) appears in human form
Humanoid	Humanoid	Intelligent elemental creature in human form, seeking specific goals, e.g. a soul or child
Animal	Fantastic Creature	Mythical creature, often with at least one unique magickal trait
Devious	Trickster	Malicious or malevolent elemental, usually has a primary and sometimes secondary form
Simple	Elemental	Simple and unintelligent elemental creature with a single function and purpose.

Classification of Air Elemental Creatures

Level	Creature	Notes
Overseer	Raphael	Archangel
Ruler	Cherub	Angelic Overseer
Aristocracy	Fir Chlis/Merry Dancers	Fairies said to be seen as the Aurora Borealis or Northern Lights
	Leanan Sidhe/Fairy Mistress	Inspirational spirit which acted as a muse for artistic types, but often at the cost of shortening their life
Humanoid	Co-Walker/Fetch	A doppelganger, who presages the death of the person he resembles
	Faun/Satyr	Lecherous forest spirit with goats legs
	Sylph	Air elemental, often seen as a translucent human
	Sylvestre/Aerie	Humanoid elemental, usually blond and very intelligent
Animal	Pegasus	Winged horse
	Roc	Giant bird
Devious	Boneless/It	Amorphous mischievous shapeshifter
Simple	Just-Halver/Joint-Eater	Invisible spirit that devours its victim's food

Classification of Fire Elemental Creatures

Level	Creature	Notes
Overseer	Michael	Archangel
Ruler	Seruph	Angelic Overseer
Aristocracy	Djinn	Commonly called genie, powerful amoral shapeshifting tricksters
Genius	Penates/Lares	Home or place based creature
Humanoid	Vulcan/Aetnean	Humanoid, usually red haired and hot tempered
Animal	Phoenix	Bird, reborn in fire every 500 years
Devious	Ignis Fatuus	Ball of fire/light seen on moors or in marshes
Simple	Salamander	Classic lizard form
	Scintilla	Belching fire

Classification of Water Elemental Creatures

Level	Creature	Notes
Overseer	Gabriel	Archangel
Ruler	Tharsis	Angelic Overseer
Aristocracy	Lake Maiden	Benevolent lake dweller
	Melusine	Shapeshifting beautiful elementals who often marry humans, often serpentine or draconian
	Mons Veneris	Name for Nymph society
Genius	Naiad	River guardian
	White/Blue Lady	Female figure associated with sacred wells or springs
Humanoid	Blue Men of Minch	Wrecker tribe of intelligent undines
	Mermaid	Not always hostile
	Seal Maiden	Beautiful women who transform by a magickal seal skin
Animal	Sea Goat	Half goat, half fish spirit
Devious	Fuath	Malicious water spirits particularly associated with fresh water sites
	Incubus/Succubus	Sexually predatory spirits which molest people at night
	Nixie	Treacherous river-dwelling beautiful women who drown men
	Siren	Lure sailors to their deaths with their song
	Water Bull	Bull which tries to kill people or steal cattle by driving them into the sea
	Water Horse	Horse which tries to kill people by luring them to ride and taking them into the sea
	Water Leaper	Malicious water spirit which jumps out of rivers to drag men and animals to their death
Simple	Sea Spirit	Water spirit propitiated with offerings for a good catch
	Undine/Nymph	May assume human form, entirely emotional and dangerously empathic

Classification of Earth Elemental Creatures

Level	Creature	Notes
Overseer	Uriel	Archangel
Ruler	Ariel	Angelic Overseer
Aristocracy	Fairy/Elf	Whole social group of amoral trickster beings, adept at glamour and magick
Genius	Brownie	House spirit, often departs on being seen
	Cughtagh	Cave spirit
	Dryad/Durdale	Tree spirit
Humanoid	Blue Cap	Mining spirit who worked with humans
	Dwarf/Gnome/Pygmy	Short hard working earth spirit
	Giant	Large and extremely strong elemental, may be positive or malicious
	Knocker	Mining spirit who could help or hinder
Animal	Black Dogs	Numerous types exist, some of which are devious
Devious	Goblin	Malicious spirit
	Kobold	Malicious mine spirit
	Ogre	Malicious cannibal spirit in human form

Sylphs of Air

"The air is full of an innumerable multitude of Peoples, whose faces are human, seemingly rather haughty, yet in reality tractable, great lovers of the sciences, cunning, obliging to the Sages, and enemies of fools and the ignorant."[31]

In appearance Sylphs are said to appear taller and with sharper features than men or women when they are in human form. They are first mentioned by Paracelsus in his writings, and he also refers to them as *Nenufareni*. The word sylph is probably derived from the word *sylvan* or *sylvain*, referring to an airy forest spirit. Paracelsus wrote that *"The sylvans are closest to us, for they too are supported by our air."*

Sylphs are best known from Alexander Pope's famous novel of 1712, *The Rape of the Lock.* In this he belittles the classical deities, equating them to sylphs, though here he may have simply been following on from De Villars, who described the classical Greek god Pan as the greatest of the sylphs. De Villars also referred to female sylphs as sylphids.

The Greek *Anemoi* (wind gods) of the four cardinal directions and four cross-quarters were depicted as winged men who could also assume the form of horses or gusts of wind. Eurus, Notus, Zephyrus and Boreas were the gods of the east, south, west and north winds respectively. The four winds of the cross-quarters also had gods, called the *Anemoi Thuellai* (tempest winds). These were Kaikias (north-east), Apeliotes (south-east), Lips (south-west) and Skiron (north-west). As shapeshifting winged airy beings, it is possible the Anemoi

---

31 Le Comte de Gabalis, de Villars, 1670.

were the origins of the sylphs. If we consider the description given by the sixteenth century German magician Abbot Johannes Trithemius, it supports this idea. Trithemius declared in his *Eight Questions*:

"The spirits of the air can descend to the earth and by assuming a body of densified air can make themselves visible to men on many occasions."[32]

Certainly the beauty of the sylphs has captivated authors for centuries, as can be seen from the writing of the nineteenth century American anthropologist Charles Godfrey Leland:

"How shall I describe ye, O beautiful Sylphs! Bright dwellers in the aerial element, how can I tell the unutterable longing, the deep yearning with which my heart inclines to your celestial company!"[33]

Another possible origin for the sylphs is the Old Testament. There are references to the winds being angels, such as in *Psalms*, where it says: *"Who maketh his angels winds; his ministers a flaming fire."*[34] Considering the image of angels as beautiful winged humans, this could easily have become the image of the sylphs. Lewis Spence supported this idea in his *Encyclopaedia of Occultism* when he wrote *"it is probable that the lesser angels of the older magicians were the sylphs of Paracelsus."*

This is further emphasised in the New Testament in the Gospel of *Luke*, when the boat bearing Jesus is in danger of sinking. The rebuke delivered by Jesus is clearly to living creatures, which appear to be elemental:

---

32 Eight Questions, Trithemius, 1515.

33 Meister Karl's Sketch-book, Leland, 1855

34 Psalms 104:4.

"And they came to him, and awoke him, saying, Master, master, we perish. Then he arose, and rebuked the wind and the raging of the water: and they ceased, and there was a calm."[35]

When a Sylph appears as a Mane (ghost), it is said to presage great want and poverty for the people in the area. Lemures (ghosts) are also seen as elemental creatures of air, being the shells of the dead using the most easily accessible element (air) to try and hold on to form.

---

35 Luke 8:23-24

Salamanders of Fire

The traditional image of the salamander is as the amphibian which it is named after, although some medieval images also showed them being somewhat doglike in size and appearance. The name comes from the Greek word *salamandra*, the meaning of which is unknown, though it has been suggested it may be associated with fireplaces. The first known written reference to the salamander occurs in the lost fourth century BCE writings of the Greek philosopher Aristotle, preserved by Cicero in *The Nature of the Gods*. Cicero recorded Aristotle as writing in *The Generation of Animals*:

"Now the salamander is a clear case in point, to show us that animals do actually exist that fire cannot destroy; for this creature, so the story goes, not only walks through the fire but puts it out in doing so."[36]

In his classic thirty-seven volume work, *Natural History*, Pliny wrote in the first century CE that the salamander *"is so intensely cold as to extinguish fire by its contact, in the same way that ice does."*[37] His views were perpetuated by the third century CE Roman naturalist Aelian, who repeated them in his *De Natura Animalium*.

St Augustine mentioned the salamander in his *City of God* in the fifth century CE, citing it as an example that fire did not always consume, and thus evidence that souls were not consumed in the flames of hell, but suffered eternal torment. In the seventh century CE, Isidore of Seville repeated the view of Pliny in *Etymologies*, that the salamander put out fire.

---

36 Generation of Animals, Aristotle, C4th BCE.
37 Natural History, Book X, Pliny, C1st CE.

The idea that salamanders put out fire may rather indicate their own fiery nature, for the best way to put out fire is with another fire. So it may be that the fire being put out by the salamander was actually being eaten by it. This idea was postulated by Leonardo Da Vinci, who suggested that they ate fire to renew their skin:

"This has no digestive organs, and gets no food but from the fire, in which it constantly renews its scaly skin. The salamander, which renews its scaly skin in the fire - for virtue."[38]

In fact the amphibians called salamanders often hibernate in rotting logs, and so the notion of salamanders appearing and disappearing in flames may arise from them being woken out of hibernation and doing their best to get out of a fire before they die!

In his *Autobiography*, the Italian Renaissance craftsman Benvenuto Cellini described seeing a salamander in the fire when he was five (in 1505). On telling his father about the lizard in the flames, his father hit him to make sure he never forgot the auspicious day, and then gave him money. Interestingly Cellini's *Autobiography* also gives one of the best examples of the detail of a demonic evocation as well.

The *Talmud* suggests that anyone anointed with the blood of a salamander would be immune to the influence of fire (*Hagiga 25a*), and this is a common theme found in a number of Jewish writings.

Also included amongst the different classes of fire elemental creature is the Scintilla or Spark, which appears as a belching fire, and whose presence presages destruction in the country where it is seen, often indicating the fall of the ruler. Paracelsus used the term *Acthnil* to describe elemental creatures of fire which appeared as balls of fire or tongues of fire.

---

38 The Notebooks of Leonardo Da Vinci, McCurdy, 1954

Undines of Water

"There are certain Water Elementals whom Orpheus calls Nereides,
dwelling in the more elevated exhalations of Water,
such as appear in damp, cloudy Air, whose bodies are sometimes seen
(as Zoroaster taught) by more acute eyes,
especially in Persia and Africa."[39]

The name undine is derived from the Latin word *unda*, meaning 'wave'. In appearance Undines are said to appear with the same stature as a woman. They tend to always have moisture in their presence, be it sweat or a humid atmosphere. Undines are sometimes called ondines, although this latter term is derived from the name of a specific water nymph in German mythology, rather than the whole class of being.

Undines were particularly noted for marrying humans and bearing children to their husbands. Of all the types of elemental creature they are most prone to this pursuit. Unfortunately this inclination also encapsulates their most tragic natures, as it inevitably it seems to end in disaster. This is illustrated in the tales of Ondine, Melusine and other watery elemental creatures found scattered throughout European mythology and folklore.

The tendency for female undines to marry male humans, which most often seem to be the case, might have something to do with the fact that there seem to be more female undines than male ones. De Villars comments on this saying:

"The ancient Sages called this race of people Undines or Nymphs.
There are very few males among them but a great number of females;

---

39 Chaldean Oracles of Zoroaster, No.77.

their beauty is extreme, and the daughters of men
are not to be compared to them."[40]

Undines are also known as Nymphs. This clearly links back to a huge range of beings in the ancient world, with Nymphs being popular figures associated with water sources in the mythologies of Greece and Rome. The term Nymph was also subsequently applied to goddesses with associations to water in the Romano-Celtic world.

When an undine is seen in the form of a Siren, it was believed to herald divisions and destruction amongst the rulers and religions of the associated country in which it did so.

---

40 Le Comte de Gabalis, de Villars, 1670.

Gnomes of Earth

*"The earth is filled well-nigh to its centre with Gnomes, people of slight
stature, who are the guardians of treasures, minerals and precious stones.
They are ingenious, friends of man and easy to govern."*[41]

The Earth Elementals are best known as Gnomes, though they
were also referred to in the Grimoires as Cubitali and as Pygmies due
to their short stature. The word gnome may be derived from the Greek
word *genomos*, meaning *'earth dweller'*. The Gnomes dwell in the earth,
and in the past were believed to often be found in mines and under
mountains, especially in places where metals and gems were mined.

Those Gnomes who dwelt in mines were sometimes known as
Knockers, due to their tendency to knock on the mine walls for various
reasons. If they knocked once, twice or thrice it was thought to
indicate a cave-in or accident, and the wise man would immediately
move to a different part of the mine. Knockers could be troublesome
when angered, but they were also known to work for wages when
befriended, being the best miners an employer could ever hope for, but
woe betide the man who tried to short-change a knocker, for he would
be beset with troubles.

*"The type of gnome most frequently seen is the brownie, or elf, a mischievous
and grotesque little creature from twelve to eighteen inches high, usually
dressed in green or russet brown. Most of them appear as very aged, often
with long white beards, and their figures are inclined to rotundity. They can
be seen scampering out of holes in the stumps of trees and sometimes they
vanish by actually dissolving into the tree itself."*[42]

---

41 Le Comte de Gabalis, de Villars, 1670.
42 Den Ældra Eddas Gudesange, Gjellerup, 1895.

In general appearance Gnomes are said to appear short, being described as being around 1m tall or less. Although considered small by nature, Gnomes can change their shape to whatever size and appearance they choose. When Gnomes appear as Giants, it usually presages great ruin or mischief in the area where they are seen. This brings us to an interesting point made in Grimoires that fairies, which are often considered to be airy and ethereal beings, are in fact part of the family of beings often referred to as Gnomes.

"Of this terrestrial order are likewise those, which are commonly called Fairies. It is Credibly Asserted, that in ancient times that many of those aforesaid Gnomes, Fairies Elves & other terrestrial wandering spirits, have been seen & heard amongst Men, but now it is said & believed that they are not so frequent."[43]

---

43 Sloane MSS 3825, C17th CE.

CHAPTER 8

Elemental Tides

Like the planets, the elements have their own times at which their powers peak and trough. The elemental cycles operate both on a daily and a seasonal basis, and may be included in your magickal work to good effect, to further enhance and refine the energy you are working with.

During the day, dawn corresponds to Air, noon to Fire, dusk to Water and midnight to Earth. Seasonally the sequence is usually viewed as Spring (Air), Summer (Fire), Autumn (Water) and Winter (Earth).

From a magickal perspective, dawn is the liminal time at the start of the day, the balance between light and dark, day and night. This makes for an excellent period to perform magickal work for new beginnings, associated with the element of Air. Likewise Spring is the time when life is emerging from the earth, beginning its growth cycle anew, and so this is also an ideal time for new projects. Thus spring dawns are the optimum time for beginning something new.

Midday is usually the time with the most light, and when we feel the most active. Our energy is in full swing and we want to get things done, so this is a time for making things grow and develop. If you need something to succeed, concentrate on it at midday at the time of

Fire. Likewise Summer is the season when flowers and plants are in full bloom and life is in its most vigorous glory, moving to fruition.

Dusk is the second liminal time of the day, when the darkness of night is overcoming the light of day. This is often considered the most magickal time of the day, when it is easiest to work magick in the gap between light and dark. It is also a particularly good time for divination. This is a good time to bring projects to a conclusion, finishing them in a state of balance. As the watery season, Autumn is a time of surprises, when the rain can appear out of nowhere, leaving the beauty of a rainbow in its place. It is a time of harvest, and so likewise is a time to finish projects.

Midnight is a time of transition, into the next day. It is the time of Earth, as the patience and strength of Earth are emphasised by the silence of night, which is an ideal time for contemplation and reflection, to look within during the moment of repose. Winter is the season of Earth, at the end of the year when life moves into dormancy, whether it is plants in the ground or people retreating into their houses. The cold and bleak weather encourages contemplation and planning, working out ideas for when the season moves into the dynamism of Air in the Spring again.

In the ancient world the tides were perceived somewhat differently, based on the qualities rather than the elements, a system which does not perhaps work as well now the weather conditions have shifted, and are not based on an ancient Mediterranean climate. Thus the summer and winter solstices corresponded to warm and cool, and the spring and autumn equinoxes to moist and dry. This gave the seasonal attributions as air (spring), fire (summer), earth (autumn) and water (winter).

Element	Time	Season
Air	Dawn	Spring
Fire	Noon	Summer
Water	Dusk	Autumn
Earth	Midnight	Winter

As the planets are higher manifestations of the elemental energies, you can also choose a day of the week which has a connection to the element you are going to work with:

Day	Planet	Element
Sunday	Sun	Fire
Monday	Moon	Water
Tuesday	Mars	Fire
Wednesday	Mercury	Air
Thursday	Jupiter	Air or Water
Friday	Venus	Earth
Saturday	Saturn	Earth

CHAPTER 9

Preparation for Ritual

Ceremony is a key part of magickal practice. A ceremony is the synergy of its component symbols, parts and principles, and this synergy is expressed through creating a sequence of focused ritual actions imbued with power. The sequence when performed forms a critical mass of intent resulting in a predetermined consequence. When a ceremony is repeated its internal power increases and it becomes a ritual. It can then be considered a sequence of sacred technology, as it develops an inherent flow which can be experienced by anyone who practices it correctly, generating repeatable results.

For any ceremony there are a number of components to be taken into account before you start. Making sure you have considered all the components ensures your ceremonies are more likely to be successful. These components are:

1. Intent

Intent is the carefully defined purpose of a sequence of actions, fuelled by the focused pure will of the practitioner and the emotional desire to see the fulfilment of the result of those actions. Any effective ceremony will have a very precise intent. You should have formulated this as your first step, as everything else about the ceremony will depend on this.

2. Timing

The elemental time of day and tide are easily determined well in advance. This will be directly related to the nature of the elemental force used, and should not be compromised on, as the tides are both daily and seasonal. Thus the daily tide is easily achievable, as is an appropriate day of the week, even if you are months away from the seasonal tide.

3. Location

Elemental magick may be performed outdoors or indoors. If you are working indoors, do you have a permanent temple space, or do you need to make a space to work in? Whether you are indoors or outdoors, you do not want to be disturbed, and you should have removed all distractions beforehand. Make sure the space that you are working in is a comfortable temperature.

4. Purification

An important consideration for magickal work is that everything you use should be purified. Anything you take into a magick circle for ritual work should have been purified. This includes mundane items you might not otherwise consider, such as your pair of glasses if you wear them. Additionally, following purification, if an item has a specific purpose, like a tool or robe, it should also have been consecrated. Consecration involves energising the item in question towards the specific purpose(s) you will be using it for.

Having a ritual bath before a ceremony is always to be recommended, and when you do so you can use appropriately scented bath oils to fragrance your bath and aid in your purification before the ceremony. After drying yourself you should put your robe on rather than clothes, and also any ritual jewellery you may be planning on wearing for the ceremony.

5. Circle & Altar

The nature of the work you perform will contribute to your choice of circle – e.g. you may wish to increase the size of the circle if you are going to be dancing ecstatically. The altar is usually placed at the centre of the circle, but you may prefer to have it at one of the cardinal points if you are concentrating on the element associated with that direction (e.g. in the west for water, etc). An altar is like a working table, it should only have items there that need to be there.

6. Symbols

Use of appropriate symbols helps focus the mind on the intent of the ceremony. Using the appropriate elemental colour for your candles and altar cloth, and having an appropriate elemental incense will all help with focusing your mind on the energy you are working with. Your robe may be white or the appropriate elemental colour as desired.

7. Tools

Your tools include your robe, magickal weapons, candles, censer & incense, lamen, altar, altar cloth. Lamens should have been made at an appropriate elemental time. The lamen is effectively either a worn amulet providing protection from a hostile entity, or a talisman attracting the attention of a positive entity. All tools should have been purified and consecrated before the ceremony.

8. Sequence

Have a clear idea in your head of the *"running order"* of your ceremony. The sequence of elemental magick given later provides an effective template. If you are performing conjurations, have copies of anything you plan on reading in clear and large easy-to-read script. Remember that working in the semi-darkness of candlelight can make it hard to read. If you have memorised the material then a script copy is still useful in case you forget the words, or just to provide you with the confidence that comes from knowing you have planned thoroughly. If you are performing invocation or evocation, have a list of questions prepared beforehand, or it is all too easy to get distracted and not cover everything you wanted to.

CHAPTER 10

The Elemental Tools

The basic working tools of the magician are elemental in their attributions and symbolism. Thus we have the wand of air, the dagger of fire, the chalice of water and the pentacle of earth. As would be expected from the nature of the elements, the tools attributed to the masculine elements, i.e. the wand and dagger, are active tools, used for directing, whereas the tools attributed to the feminine elements, the cup and pentacle, are passive tools, used for receiving.

Tool	Wand	Dagger	Chalice	Pentacle
Element	Air	Fire	Water	Earth
Power	Direction	Control	Reception	Protection
Concept	Creativity	Will	Perception	Manifestation

Dagger

The dagger, forged of iron in the flames of the furnace, is the fire tool par excellence. In the tradition of Greek manuscripts known as *Hygromantia*, which are the precursors to the *Key of Solomon*, the instructions for the creation of the black-handled knife often require the timing to be during the hour of Mars on the day of Mars.[44] As a fiery planet, this fits entirely with the attribution of Fire. Furthermore, although it may seem extreme to us now, the instruction was that the blade should be created from an existing knife or sword that had been used to kill someone.[45]

The dagger is used to enforce the will of the magician. This is why it is used to demarcate the edge of the magick circle, and it is used to control spiritual creatures. According to the Grimoires most angels and demons have bodies made from a rarefied form of air. The significance of airy bodies is that iron weapons cleave through air. Remember the original elemental oppositions of air and earth. Iron, though forged by fire, is drawn from within the earth, and is able to cause pain to a spiritual creature with a less tangible body it passes through. This is why fairy creatures really do not like iron, and why the Grimoires insist on the magus using a sword to command the various spiritual creatures. It is for this reason that you should have at least a dagger to hand when you work magick.

We advocate the use of a double-edged black-handled knife as the fire dagger. This design is a functional and effective design, which can be engraved or marked according to the will of the magician.

Wand

The wand is the tool of air, representing the creative power of the mind. Continuing to study the instructions in manuscripts, many of the extant *Key of Solomon* manuscripts give clear instructions for the wand to be made on a Wednesday during the hour of Mercury.

---

44 This is seen in several manuscripts, such as Atheniensis MSS 1265.
45 See, e.g. Harley MSS 5596, the 15th century Greek text.

Mercury is the airy planet, in contrast to Mars, clearly reinforcing the airy nature of the wand as a tool. The length given for the wand is normally the old measurement of a cubit, i.e. from the fingertips to the elbow (usually about 18″ or 45cm).

Traditionally the wand is made from a piece of hazel or wood from another nut or fruit bearing tree, cut with a single stroke. This emphasis on the ability to produce fresh growth emphasises the creative nature of the wand. Whilst the magician commands with a dagger, with a wand they create. This is why we use the wand for consecrations when a tool is required, rather than a dagger.

Significantly, the marking of sacred words on the wand may be found as far back as the *Greek Magical Papyri*, and also with gods and animal figures on ancient Egyptian ivory apotropaic wands. In the ancient world the wand was often considered the most significant magickal tool of the magician.

Whilst there is a huge range of conflicting information about wands, and what they should be made of, and whether they should have a core of some sort, we advocate the standard Solomonic wand, of the fingertip to elbow length, made from a piece of hazel which should be no more than an inch (2.5cm) in diameter at the end you hold.

The wand may taper to a narrower end, though this does not need to be turned into a sharpened point, as the wand is not a weapon. Once the hazel has been cut, it should be stripped of the bark and oiled with an oil like linseed or olive oil to preserve it. After a few days you can then carve suitable symbols on it.

Pentacle

The pentacle or disk is the symbol of earth. Its solid shape and form leave no doubt of this. However, again it is not really utilised to its full measure. The pentacles seen in the Grimoires are effectively talismans made of planetary metals (or in some instances woods) and worn by the magician to exert control over a spiritual creature or to achieve a desired result. This form of practical magick has largely been left behind as being an anachronism of the past, for which we may more accurately say, too much like hard work!

Thus a pentacle represents the ultimate power of earth as manifestation, providing a magickal shield emblazoned with protective symbols appropriate to the work you are performing. This is why in the *Key of Solomon* it says:

"The Pentacle is the principle instrument of the Art because without it, you cannot perform any Operation. All power and virtue are contained in it. It is through this that all the Spirits, good or evil are forced to obey and to come when the person performing the Operation commands them."

The Pentacle design we recommend is based on one of the Jupiterian pentacles from the *Key of Solomon*, being an equal-armed cross in a circle, with the names of the four elemental rulers in the arms. In the centre is a hexagram representing the universe, and also containing the four elemental triangles. In the outer rim of the pentacle are pentagrams at the east, south and west, and the symbol for Ariel as the elemental ruler of Earth in the north.

The Pentacle

Cup

The chalice or cup is clearly a watery tool. Its primary function is to hold liquid, be this wine, water or something else. Whilst the chalice may have now been relegated to the position of symbolic drinking vessel, in the past it was a key tool, being the focus for hydromancy, or divination by liquid. This practice was frequently used for conjuring angels, demons and planetary creatures for communication, and can be seen as parallel to the use of other mediums such as a mirror or crystal. However a range of influences caused magick to move to a perception which requires the physical manifestation of entities. This has sadly resulted in a move away from appreciating the reality of spiritual creatures and interacting with them, rather adopting the paradigm of seeing them as useful psychological constructs which can assist in the process of self-development or *'self-empowerment'*.

Altar

One of the most important items for the temple as a tool, though it is passive in that it is not moved, is the altar. Of course it could be argued that it is a piece of furniture rather than a tool, but that is up to you to decide. The ideal design for the altar is the classic double cube design. This form embodies the glyph of the Tree of Life as an elemental design. The Tree of Life is a design of ten spheres (the Sephiroth) joined by twenty-two paths, forming a multi-levelled glyph which represents both the universe and the human body. The Sephiroth are formed by a process of manifestation from the undivided divine at Kether through to the manifestation of the physical realm at Malkuth.

The top and bottom represent Kether and Malkuth as the two Sephiroth containing all the elements (Sephiroth 1 and 10). Kether as the divine manifestation is the upper surface where the magician places the tools of the art, and Malkuth as the lower surface is the plane of contact with the physical world through the floor.

The four rectangular sides, each being two squares one on top of the other, then represent the other eight Sephiroth in their elemental attributions as two of each of the four elements. Thus the sides are Air (Chokmah and Hod, Sephiroth 2 and 8), Fire (Geburah and Tiphereth,

Sephiroth 5 and 6), Water (Chesed and Yesod, Sephiroth 4 and 9) and Earth (Binah and Netzach, Sephiroth 3 and 7). The division between the upper and lower cubes also represents the elements within and without. The upper cube has the higher elemental powers corresponding to the journey from the planet Earth out of the solar system, representing the radiation of magick into the world, whereas the lower cube has the elemental powers corresponding to the inward journey from the Earth in to the Sun, representing the magickal balancing of the self.

It could also be argued that the inside of the altar, where tools are stored, symbolises Daath as the repository of knowledge through the focal action of the tools as weapons of intent to achieve magickal results.

Elemental Tool Consecration

The act of consecrating your ceremonial tools is one of the most important things you will perform as part of your preparatory workings. It is through consecration that you assign a purpose to the tool, whilst also declaring it as magical and sacred. So for example within the context of elemental magick, prior to consecration your Fire Dagger is just a knife, but after it has been properly consecrated it becomes the elemental tool of Fire.

For this consecration we use the following symbols for each of the four elements. They represent the four elements, and the duplication of the symbol within the symbol hints at the power controlling the element, i.e. the elemental governor. You can if you prefer use the common elemental triangles instead.

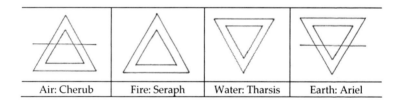

| Air: Cherub | Fire: Seraph | Water: Tharsis | Earth: Ariel |

Hold the tool in your preferred hand in the direction associated with the element of the tool.

Proclaim:

I consecrate thee [tool] in the name of the archangel [name] that you be a holy implement for my will, and serve me [magickal name] as a potent and effective emblem of the element of [element] by the power of the elemental governor [governor name].

Now hold the tool to your heart for four heartbeats, feeling the strength of your link to the tool, and its function as an extension of your intent.

Next engrave the symbol of the elemental governor on your tool. For a wand carve this on the base (i.e. the circular bottom), for the dagger on the blade by the handle, for the chalice on the base, and for the pentacle in the top of the circle.

When you have finished hold the tool in your preferred hand in the direction associated with the element again.

Proclaim:

I consecrate thee anew in the name of the archangel [name] that you serve me [magickal name] in all my deeds, visible and invisible, in every realm, as a potent and effective emblem of the element of [element] by the power of the elemental governor [governor name].

Tool	Wand	Dagger	Chalice	Pentacle
Archangel	Raphael	Michael	Gabriel	Uriel
Element	Air	Fire	Water	Earth
Governor	Cherub	Seraph	Tharsis	Ariel

CHAPTER 11

The Magick Circle of the Four Elements

In every respect the magick circle is a place of balance. It symbolises the focal essence of the magician's intent, as a nexus for change, a liminal place of transition between force and form where intent is realised. It is created by the magician to be a space in which to perform magickal and sometimes also spiritual work. The magick circle can as such rightly be described as one of the most important parts of any ritual work.

The magick circle serves as a demarcation between the magickal space created by the magician, and the mundane world. Because the magick circle is balanced between so many different possible forces, it is essential that it is created as a place of harmony. The magick circle must be created with the full attention and intent of the magician, as a place of grace, truth and power. By so doing the magician not only sets up the necessary dynamic required for effective direction of power, but also creates a purity which can be used to attract the attention of the spiritual creatures you seek. The level of respect for the spiritual creatures and self-worth of the magician can both be read from the purity and truth of the intent in the heart and mind of the magician.

The elemental magick circle is created using the elements, specifically as a place for practising elemental magick, although it can also be used for other forms of magick, representing as it does creation from the simplest component parts.

Creating your Elemental Circle

You will be creating a circle which will be 9 foot (2.7m) in diameter. The purpose of this circle is to create a magickal space for performing your elemental magick in.

You will need:
- A small bowl containing water (preferably living water).
- A censer of incense
- Spirit light (lamp or a candle)
- Taper or candle

For the creation of the circle you may use a dagger, or your preferred hand. If you use your hand, make the gesture of benediction. This is made by extending the forefinger and big finger, and curling the ring finger and little finger into the palm, with the thumb curled over so it rests on the ring and little fingers.

The idea of enkindling water by placing a brand in it to make it holy can be found in ancient Greek ceremonies for the creation of *húdôr theíon* ('holy water'), also known in Latin as *aqua igne sacra inflammata* ('water inflamed by sacred fire').

Before the ceremony commences light the spirit light and the charcoal block.

Light the taper from your spirit flame.

Dip the taper flame into the water, extinguishing it. As you do so, proclaim:

I [magickal name] enkindle this water with my will. Fire and water united create the sacred conjunction of opposites, and from this is holiness born. The rising fire descends, the descending water rises, as above, so below.

Put the taper down on the altar, then pick up the bowl of consecrated water and walk around the space, starting in the East, in a clockwise circle, sprinkling the consecrated water as you walk. When you have returned to the East, go back to the altar and replace the bowl on the altar.

Add incense to the charcoal block. As you do so, proclaim:

I [magickal name] transform this earth with my will. Through the medium of fire, earth becomes air and the sweet fragrance of sacredness is released. The intangible air manifests, the manifest earth sublimates, as above, so below.

Pick up the censer of incense (frankincense is ideal as a general incense, though of course you may use a specific blended elemental incense or appropriately attributed resin) and return to the East, walking in a clockwise circle, censing with the incense as you walk. When you have returned to the East, go back to the altar, replace the censer on the altar and make the gesture of benediction.

Again go to the East and walk clockwise around your space with your arm outstretched downwards towards the floor and see a circle of white flames being formed at the tip of the weapon or your fingers, and say:

United and conjoined the four elemental powers
form the greater unity,
That unity is my magick circle, bound in time and space
Within is my universe
harmonised by the magick of the elements.
As above, so below

When you have returned to the East, return to the centre and place your weapon on the altar, and continue with your ceremony.

CHAPTER 12

The Elemental Pyramids

As we mentioned previously in our work *Practical Planetary Magick*, the pyramids came about as a result of inspiration for a magickal group we were (and continue to be) involved with. The Spirit pyramid was the first one, which then led to the four Elemental pyramids, and the subsequent manifestation of the Planetary pyramids. The sequence is easy to memorise, and if you struggle with recall, simply write down the key points like the mantra and the qualities for each direction on a piece of paper which you can refer to if you forget. You will soon find the qualities stuck firmly in your mind. As with other meditational work, do not feel you need to hurry through them. Take your time and ensure you receive the full benefits of the elemental qualities when you perform them.

This has proved to be a very useful preparatory technique for magickal work, focusing the practitioner on the energy appropriate to the work being conducted. The pyramids can be used as stand-alone exercises for developing your connection with the elements, or for strengthening elemental qualities within yourself. They work well for the process of enhancing positive or transforming negative qualities, particularly if used in conjunction with the elemental temples. Ideally the pyramids should be used over a period of days or weeks for such work, do not expect overnight results from a single use.

You can of course use the pyramids for other energy work, such as generating and focusing elemental energy for consecration or purification; it is a very adaptable technique. The pyramids also work well for both solitary practice and group work, which they were originally created for.

Experience has shown a number of phenomenon associated with the elemental pyramids, which you may experience when you practice them. The Air pyramid may be accompanied by a feeling of breeze, as the air in the room seems to develop its own circulatory system, even in closed spaces; additionally you may hear whispers or smell unexpected fragrances. The Fire pyramid may be accompanied by a feeling of increased heat and dryness, as if all moisture has been extracted from the room; additionally you may feel hotter as your body temperature increases and begin sweating. The Water pyramid may be accompanied by a feeling of increased moisture, as if the level of water vapour in the room has increased noticeably; additionally you may feel a chill and clamminess, and in extreme cases start to salivate. The Earth pyramid may be accompanied by a feeling of heaviness and solidity, as if you are in a cavern deep underground, with sounds seeming to echo and resonate more than usual; additionally you may feel a sense of strength or calm filling you.

The Aether pyramid may be accompanied by a feeling of elation or sudden insight, and you may feel a sense of sharp focus or clear-headedness which brings all your plans into relief.

The Air Pyramid

The word used as a mantra in this pyramid is *Gnosis*, the Greek for *'Knowledge'*. The form of knowledge expressed by gnosis is spiritual knowledge, obtained through direct experience of altered states of consciousness and interaction with other beings and other realms. The colour of sky blue is used throughout the visualisation as the colour seen when looking at the sky.

The qualities we attributed to the corners of the pyramid are clarity, inspiration, joy and wisdom, and their airy nature is emphasised in the accompanying visualisations of the feather, cloud, disk and scales.

Air Pyramid Working

See yourself sitting in a sky blue square within the circle, whose corners are in the East, South, West and North, touching the edge of the circle. This square symbolises the power of the Air. In the first corner, in the East, is the first of the four powers of the Air, that of clarity. See the energy of clarity as a sky blue feather in the eastern corner, glowing with an inner vibrancy as it embodies the clarity of the beliefs and practices that you live by. Concentrate on focusing the energy of clarity in the eastern corner of the square.

Clarity produces realisation and inspiration, which is not static, so move the clarity to the second corner of the square, in the South. Do this with the word Gnosis. Chant Gnosis four times to send the energy of clarity down the sky blue edge of the square to the southern corner.

GNOSIS (x4)

In the second corner in the South, clarity is transformed into the second quality of the Air, that of inspiration. Inspiration gives form to the unseen, manifesting your ideas into a form that can be carried forward. Focus on transforming the energy of clarity into inspiration at the second corner of the square, in the South, visualising the sky blue feather changing into a white cloud on a sky blue background.

Now move the power of inspiration to the third corner of the square, in the West. Do this again with the word Gnosis, chanting it four times to send the energy of inspiration down the sky blue edge of the square to the western corner.

GNOSIS (x4)

In the third corner in the West, inspiration is transformed into joy, the third quality of the Air. Joy is an expression of clarity and inspiration, the joy of doing the right actions, taking pleasure in your life and path. See the cloud on the sky blue background change into a sky blue disk, radiating sky blue rays outwards. Focus on gathering the energy of joy in the third corner of the square, in the West.

Joy spreads, so move it to the fourth corner of the square, in the North. To do this chant the word Gnosis four times to send the energy of joy down the sky blue edge of the square to the northern corner.

GNOSIS (x4)

In the North joy is transformed into the fourth quality of the Air, that of wisdom. Wisdom comes from finding joy in your clarity and inspiration, and understanding the flow of life around you and its balance. See the sky blue solar disk change into a sky blue pair of scales. Focus on transforming that joy you have moved here into wisdom.

To complete the square move the wisdom to the eastern corner by chanting Gnosis four times, to send the energy of wisdom down the sky blue edge of the square to the eastern corner.

GNOSIS (x4)

Now you sit within the sky blue square of the Air, with its powers of clarity, inspiration, joy and wisdom. To use these qualities you must move in time, which means you need to transform the square into three dimensions. Visualise a sky blue line rising from each of the four corners, to meet in the centre above you, forming a pyramid. As you are completing the pyramid, use the phrase Gnosis to express the triumph of life in its myriad forms. So chant Gnosis four times to aid the formation of the pyramid as you see the lines rising to the upper central point.

GNOSIS (x4)

Now you sit inside the pyramid of the Air, in the inner chamber. You are surrounded by the sky blue energies of clarity and inspiration, of joy and wisdom. Draw those sky blue energies into your heart so that your body and aura are permeated with the sky blue power of the Air. Do this until all the energy is absorbed and the pyramid has faded away.

The Fire Pyramid

The word used as a mantra in this pyramid is *Ashim*, the Hebrew for *'Flames'* (not being used here as the name of the Qabalistic angels of the Sephira of Malkuth). Flames with their ever-changing dancing forms embody the power of Fire and so this is an ideal mantra to represent the element. The colour of red is used throughout the visualisation as the colour seen when looking at the heart of fire. The qualities we attributed to the corners of the pyramid are illumination, drive, creativity and power, and their fiery nature is emphasised in the accompanying visualisations of the solar disk, lightning flash, lava and lion.

Fire Pyramid Working

See yourself sitting in a red square within the circle, whose corners are in the East, South, West and North, touching the edge of the circle. This square symbolises the power of the Fire. In the first corner, in the East, is the first of the four powers of the Fire, that of illumination. See the energy of illumination as a red solar disk in the eastern corner, glowing with the illuminating light of the rising sun. Concentrate on focusing the energy of illumination in the eastern corner of the square.

Illumination produces the drive for action, which is not static, so move the illumination to the second corner of the square, in the South. Do this with the word Ashim. Chant Ashim four times to send the energy of illumination down the red edge of the square to the southern corner.

ASHIM (x4)

In the second corner in the South, illumination is transformed into the second quality of the Fire, that of drive. Drive carries you forward on your path, fuelling your thoughts and deeds. Focus on transforming the energy of illumination into drive at the second corner of the square, in the South, visualising the red solar disk changing into a red lightning flash.

Now move the power of drive to the third corner of the square, in the West. Do this again with the word Ashim, chanting it four times to send the energy of drive down the red edge of the square to the western corner.

ASHIM (x4)

In the third corner in the West, drive is transformed into creativity, the third quality of the Fire. Creativity expresses your drive and illumination, producing new forms or refining existing ones, moving ideas and practices forward. See the red lightning flash change into a red river of lava, radiating heat and light outwards. Focus on gathering the energy of creativity in the third corner of the square, in the West.

Creativity creates action, so move it to the fourth corner of the square, in the North. To do this chant the word Ashim four times to send the energy of creativity down the red edge of the square to the northern corner.

ASHIM (x4)

In the North creativity is transformed into the fourth quality of Fire, that of power. Power comes from your own drives and creativity, and is expressed into the world through the illumination of your words and deeds. See the red river of lava change into a red lion. Focus on transforming that creativity you have moved here into power.

To complete the square move the power to the eastern corner by chanting Ashim four times, to send the energy of power down the red edge of the square to the eastern corner.

ASHIM (x4)

Now you sit within the red square of Fire, with its powers of illumination, drive, creativity and power. To use these qualities you must move in time, which means you need to transform the square into three dimensions. Visualise a red line rising from each of the four corners, to meet in the centre above you, forming a pyramid. As you are completing the pyramid, use the phrase Ashim to express the power of Fire in its myriad forms. So chant Ashim four times to aid the formation of the pyramid as you see the lines rising to the upper central point.

ASHIM (x4)

Now you sit inside the pyramid of the Fire, in the inner chamber. You are surrounded by the red energies of creativity and drive, of illumination and power. Draw those red energies into your heart so that your body and aura are permeated with the red power of Fire. Do this until all the energy is absorbed and the pyramid has faded away.

The Water Pyramid

The word used as a mantra in this pyramid is *Hudor*, the Greek for *'Water'*. The colour of deep blue is used throughout the visualisation as the colour seen when looking at the deep sea.

The qualities we attributed to the corners of the pyramid are empathy, intuition, compassion and serenity, and their watery nature is emphasised in the accompanying visualisations of a river, a waterfall, a tear and a still lake.

Water Pyramid Working

See yourself sitting in a deep blue square within the circle, whose corners are in the East, South, West and North, touching the edge of the circle. This square symbolises the power of Water. In the first corner, in the East, is the first of the four powers of Water, that of empathy. See the energy of empathy as a deep blue river in the eastern corner, carrying the empathic power of your being. Concentrate on focusing the energy of empathy in the eastern corner of the square.

Empathy produces intuitive realisation, and with realisation comes movement, so move the empathy to the second corner of the square, in the South. Do this with the word Hudor. Chant Hudor four times to send the energy of empathy down the deep blue edge of the square to the southern corner.

HUDOR (x4)

In the second corner in the South, empathy is transformed into the second quality of Water, that of intuition. Intuition connects disparate parts of your being, forming a bridge between your unconscious and superconscious mind. Focus on transforming the energy of empathy into intuition at the second corner of the square, in the South, visualising the deep blue river becoming a waterfall.

Now move the power of intuition to the third corner of the square, in the West. Do this again with the word Hudor, chanting it four times to send the energy of intuition down the deep blue edge of the square to the western corner.

HUDOR (x4)

In the third corner in the West, drive is transformed into compassion, the third quality of Water. Compassion expresses your ability to relate to and love the rest of existence, showing your awareness of the interconnectedness of the tides of life. See the deep blue waterfall change into a single deep blue tear, brimming with compassion. Focus on gathering the energy of compassion in the third corner of the square, in the West.

Compassion presages serenity, so move it to the fourth corner of the square, in the North. To do this chant the word Hudor four times to send the energy of compassion down the deep blue edge of the square to the northern corner.

HUDOR (x4)

In the North compassion is transformed into the fourth quality of Water, that of serenity. Serenity is a peace where harmony has been achieved through balance of the emotions and other qualities. See the deep blue tear form into a still lake. Focus on transforming that compassion you have moved here into serenity.

To complete the square move the serenity to the eastern corner by chanting Hudor four times, to send the energy of serenity down the deep blue edge of the square to the eastern corner.

HUDOR (x4)

Now you sit within the deep blue square of Water, with its powers of illumination, drive, creativity and power. To use these qualities you must move in time, which means you need to transform the square into three dimensions. Visualise a deep blue line rising from each of the four corners, to meet in the centre above you, forming a pyramid. As you are completing the pyramid, use the phrase Hudor to express the power of Water in its myriad forms. So chant Hudor four times to aid the formation of the pyramid as you see the lines rising to the upper central point.

HUDOR (x4)

Now you sit inside the pyramid of Water, in the inner chamber. You are surrounded by the deep blue energies of empathy and intuition, of compassion and serenity. Draw those deep blue energies into your heart so that your body and aura are permeated with the deep blue power of Water. Do this until all the energy is absorbed and the pyramid has faded away.

The Earth Pyramid

The word used as a mantra in this pyramid is *Aretz*, the Hebrew for *'Earth'*. The colour of green is used throughout the visualisation as the colour in nature of vegetative life.

The qualities we attributed to the corners of the pyramid are patience, steadfastness, responsibility and strength, and their earthy nature is emphasised in the accompanying visualisations of an oak tree, a grass-covered hill, a paved stone road, and a black bull.

Earth Pyramid Working

See yourself sitting in a green square within the circle, whose corners are in the East, South, West and North, touching the edge of the circle. This square symbolises the power of Earth. In the first corner, in the East, is the first of the four powers of Earth, that of patience. See the energy of patience as a large oak tree, its leaves green, in the eastern corner, representing your patience. Concentrate on focusing the energy of patience in the eastern corner of the square.

Patience produces fruit, like the acorns from an oak, as it grows steadfast and strong. With that growth comes movement, so move the patience to the second corner of the square, in the South. Do this with the word Aretz. Chant Aretz four times to send the energy of patience down the green edge of the square to the southern corner.

ARETZ (x4)

In the second corner in the South, patience is transformed into the second quality of Earth, that of steadfastness. Steadfastness is fixedness of purpose and loyalty to that purpose. Focus on transforming the energy of patience into steadfastness at the second corner of the square, in the South, visualising the green oak tree becoming a grass-covered hill.

Now move the power of steadfastness to the third corner of the square, in the West. Do this again with the word Aretz, chanting it four times to send the energy of steadfastness down the green edge of the square to the western corner.

ARETZ (x4)

In the third corner in the West, steadfastness is transformed into responsibility, the third quality of Earth. Responsibility expresses your ability to own your actions and carry out your duty. See the green hill change into a paved stone road leading into the distance. Focus on gathering the energy of responsibility in the third corner of the square, in the West.

Accepting responsibility shows strength and maturity, a moving forward in life, so move the responsibility to the fourth corner of the square, in the North. To do this chant the word Aretz four times to send the energy of responsibility down the green edge of the square to the northern corner.

ARETZ (x4)

In the North responsibility is transformed into the fourth quality of Earth, that of strength. Strength is a quality expressed through the different areas of your being, and always denotes hard work. See the road change into a black bull, standing strong and proud. Focus on transforming that responsibility you have moved here into strength.

To complete the square move the strength to the eastern corner by chanting Aretz four times, sending the energy of strength down the green edge of the square to the eastern corner.

ARETZ (x4)

Now you sit within the green square of Earth, with its powers of illumination, drive, creativity and power. To use these qualities you must move in time, which means you need to transform the square into three dimensions. Visualise a green line rising from each of the four corners, to meet in the centre above you, forming a pyramid. As you are completing the pyramid, use the phrase Aretz to express the power of Earth in its myriad forms. So chant Aretz four times to aid the formation of the pyramid as you see the lines rising to the upper central point.

ARETZ (x4)

Now you sit inside the pyramid of Earth, in the inner chamber. You are surrounded by the green energies of patience and steadfastness, of responsibility and strength. Draw those green energies into your heart so that your body and aura are permeated with the green power of Earth. Do this until all the energy is absorbed and the pyramid has faded away.

The Pyramid of Aether

The Aether pyramid is the final pyramid, combining the virtues of the four elemental pyramids. It was actually the first of the pyramids we created for this technique, which is one of the reasons it is somewhat different to the rest of them. Additionally of course, it is Aether, which is unique and distinct anyway.

There is a different mantra for each side of the pyramid. These are the mantras used in the elemental pyramids, being *Gnosis, Ashim, Hudor* and *Aretz*. The colours used are those of the elemental pyramids, i.e. sky blue, red, deep blue and green. This pyramid is also the only one which uses more than one colour, and it requires more effort to visualise, but it does symbolise the balance of elements required to achieve aether, so this is entirely appropriate.

The qualities we attributed to the corners of the pyramid are those of the four magickal axioms of Knowledge, Will, Daring and Silence, expressed as the elemental tools of the wand, dagger, chalice and pentacle.

Aether Pyramid Working

See yourself sitting in a white square within the circle, whose corners are in the East, South, West and North, touching the edge of the circle. This square symbolises the power of Earth. In the first corner, in the East, is the power of Air, that of knowledge. See the energy of knowledge as a caduceus, its black and white serpents entwined around the central rod, and with a winged disk at the top. Concentrate on focusing the energy of knowledge in the eastern corner of the square.

In order to Know we must will, applying ourselves to the study and experience of the universe and ourselves. With that knowledge comes growth, so move the knowledge to the second corner of the square, in the South. Do this with the word Gnosis. Chant Gnosis four times to send the energy of patience down the white edge of the square to the southern corner, turning it sky blue as you move the energy.

GNOSIS (x4)

In the second corner in the South, knowledge is transformed into the power of Fire, that of Will. To Will is to focus the inner purpose that expresses our mental strength and resolve. Concentrate on transforming the energy of knowledge into will at the second corner of the square, in the South, visualising the caduceus becoming a black-handled dagger.

Now move the power of will to the third corner of the square, in the West. Do this with the word Ashim, chanting it four times to send the energy of will down the white edge of the square to the western corner. As the energy moves, see the white edge of the square becoming red with the power of will.

ASHIM (x4)

In the third corner in the West, will is transformed into daring, the power of Water. To Dare is to use the will and have the determination to reach for your dreams and aspirations, to be true to yourself. See the black-handled dagger change into a silver chalice. Focus on gathering the energy of daring in the third corner of the square, in the West.

Daring requires balance and the inner harmony and silence of the focused mind. Move the energy of daring to the fourth corner of the square, in the North. To do this chant the word Hudor four times to send the energy of daring down the white edge of the square to the northern corner. As the energy moves down the edge see it turn deep blue.

HUDOR (x4)

In the North daring is transformed into the fourth power, of Earth, that of silence. To Keep Silent requires keeping our own counsel and stilling the chatter in our minds. Silence is a difficult virtue to find and should be cultivated. See the chalice change into a pentacle bearing a pentagram. Focus on transforming the daring you moved here into the power of silence.

To complete the square move the silence to the eastern corner by chanting Aretz four times, sending the energy of silence down the white edge of the square to the eastern corner, and seeing it turn green as it moves there.

ARETZ (x4)

Now you sit within the base of the Pyramid of Power, of the balanced elements of Air, Fire, Water and Earth, with their powers of To Know, To Will, To Dare and To Keep Silence. To use these powers you must move in time and Become, which means you need to transform the square into three dimensions. Visualise an appropriately coloured line rising from each of the four corners, to meet in the centre above you, forming a pyramid (sky blue from the east, red from the south, deep blue from the west and green from the north). As you are completing the pyramid, use the phrase *Theos Hypsistos*, (which means 'Highest God' in Greek,) to express the power of Aether. Chant Theos Hypsistos four times to aid the formation of the pyramid as you see the lines rising to the upper central point. Each line will be the same as the base line running from it clockwise, so you should see the whole side of the pyramid being the colour of the lines. Thus the east-south face will be sky blue, the south-west face will be red, the west-north face will be deep blue, and the north-east face will be green.

THEOS HYPSISTOS (x4)

Now you sit inside the pyramid of Aether, in the inner chamber. You are surrounded by the powers of the magus. Draw those energies into your heart so that your body and aura are permeated with the elemental powers. Through their balance feel your inner being growing stronger and the fibres of your being becoming more resilient and brilliant. Do this until all the energy is absorbed and the pyramid has faded away.

CHAPTER 13

The Elemental Temples

The elemental temples are places you can visit to work elemental magick. When you work with an element, you have the choice of bringing a stream of elemental force here, or of visiting an astral interface between the pure elemental realm and this one. If you choose the latter, it makes more sense to use a constructed elemental temple rather than wandering the elemental realm. With an elemental temple you have the parameters of your elemental connection much more firmly under control, removing the random factor that might otherwise intrude if you are in a changeable elemental realm.

This is not to say that elemental temples are always empty. You may find that the elemental archangel is present when you arrive or decides to turn up. This is usually announced by the sound of a bell ringing. Likewise it is not unknown for the elemental rulers to make an appearance, you are a guest in their realm, after all. If a spiritual creature does appear in your temple, you can be assured it will be of the nature of that element, and will be at worst indifferent, and at best very helpful.

The elemental temples work very well as locations for working personal change, transforming negative qualities to positive ones. They are also very good places to develop your relationships with spiritual creatures, providing a space they are comfortable with. If you are working magick to create change in a situation in the physical world, such as for a job, to pass an exam, etc, it is better to work in the physical world and bring the appropriate elemental energy into your elemental magick circle.

Visiting an elemental temple is an easy process. It can be done by using an astral doorway to start and finish the journey. This is a simple process and consists of the creation of a mental doorway to the appropriate astral realm, as described in the next section.

Temple: Inwards & Outwards

Sit comfortably facing the direction attributed to the element. Close your eyes and relax, spending a minute or two making sure you feel as comfortable and relaxed as you can. Focus on your breathing, and be aware of the breath entering and leaving your body. When you feel relaxed and your mind is focused, in your mind's eye visualise the elemental triangle for the element, on a black background in front of you. Visualise it so it is as tall as a door, and see the inside of the triangle shimmering with light the same colour as the edges of the triangle, like a curtain of coloured light.

Then in your mind's eye see yourself stand up and walk through the middle of the triangle, and find yourself in the elemental temple, standing next to the altar on the opposite side of the altar to the direction you are facing, e.g. if you enter the Temple of the Winds, you appear on the west side of the altar facing east across the altar.

Temple	Face	Triangle	Enter Temple
Winds	East	Yellow	West
Flame	South	Red	North
Water	West	Blue	East
Earth	North	Green	South

Once you appear in the temple the doorway will disappear behind you. When you wish to leave the temple and return to the mundane world, simply stand on the opposite side of the altar to the one you arrived at (i.e. the side which is the direction associated with the element) and see the elemental triangle appear directly in front of you in the same manner as you did previously, seeing it the same colour with the shimmering curtain of light in, and of a size large enough to easily walk through. You may well find this easier in the temple. Once it has appeared step through and back into your body. Take a few moments to relax again, and then open your eyes.

Temple: The Four Winds

You see that you are standing in an octagonal temple 10m across. The walls are made of white marble and extend upwards 8m. Below you the floor is a single piece of white marble. Overhead you can see the sky as there is no roof in the temple. In the north on the wall is a large frieze of a winged purple man with shaggy hair and a beard, bearing a conch shell in his hands and wearing a billowing cloak. You realise this is a depiction of Boreas, god of the north wind. On the eastern wall is a frieze showing a winged bearded man holding a heavy cloak, that you realise is Eurus. On the southern wall is a frieze depicting a winged man pouring water from a vase, which is Notus. On the western wall is a frieze showing a beardless winged youth scattering flowers from his mantle, and you realise this is Zephyrus.

Looking at the centre of the room you see there is a raised circular dias, which rises about 30cm up from the floor, and is 3m in diameter, there are four white marble pillars set at the edges of the dias so that they are in the north-east, south-east, south-west and north-west, and all equidistant from the centre. The pillars stand 3m high, and are connected by ropes at the top, joining the north-east to south-west and south-east to north-west, and forming an X in the air above the centre of the temple. From the centre of the X hangs a set of large brass wind chimes, which jingle as a wind blows through the temple. In the centre of the dias stands a white marble double-cube altar, 1m high and with a 50cm square top.

Temple: Flame

You see that you are standing in a tetrahedral temple whose sides form an equilateral triangular base with walls 10m long. The floor is made of black solidified lava, and the walls, which are made of red carnelian, meet in a triangular apex about 8.5m in the air above the centre of the temple. In the centre of the temple, about 3m from the centre of the south wall, is a double cube altar 1m high with a 0.5m square top, made from a single piece of ruby. On top of the altar is a small gold bowl, with an intense white flame burning in it.

Between the altar and the north point, about 2.5m away, is a hole in the floor. As you approach you see it is about 1m in diameter, and extends down about 20m into the earth. Looking down you see a river of molten lava is flowing under the temple, casting a fiery orange glow on the walls of the pit. Heat emanates upwards from the lava, filling the temple and giving it a very dry warm air.

As you look around the temple you see a bolt of lightning shoot down from the roof point into the bowl of white fire. Looking up you see a copper pole coming through the apex of the roof, and realise that it is a lightning conductor, bringing the power of the lightning from outside into the temple to be harnessed at the altar.

The Water Temple

You see that you are standing on a circular marble floor 10m in diameter. In the centre is a double-cube altar 1m high and 0.5m across carved from a single piece of blue sapphire. On top of the altar sits a silver bowl containing pure water, and a conch shell sits next to it. Around you the wall is made of aquamarine and rises up about 5m and then curves into a dome over the temple. Painted onto the sea green-blues of the aquamarine walls are frescos of mermaids and mermen, sea-goats, dolphins, fish and sea monsters, making a stunning mural of the denizens of the sea.

In the cardinal directions, you see four white marble pillars by the walls. The pillars are 1m wide and rise from the floor to the ceiling, standing directly in front of the walls. As you look at the pillars you realise they have water dripping down their sides, collecting in grooves at their bases and running away towards the altar, where they disappear underneath it. Looking to the west of the temple, you see what looks like a small fountain of water coming from the ground about 3m to the west of the altar. Moving closer you realise there is a hole about 1m across in the marble base, containing a small pool with a spring bubbling up fresh water.

The Earth Temple

You see that you are standing in a temple which is 10m square. Beneath your feet the ground is made from green streaked jade, as are the walls which enclose the temple. The walls rise 10m and then a flat ceiling made of lapis lazuli encloses you. In the centre of the temple is a double-cube altar 1m high and 50cm across carved from a single piece of emerald. On top of the altar sits a metallic rose, carved from a piece of magnetite.

In the corners of the temple, in the north-east, south-east, south-west and north-west are four black onyx pillars, which rise from floor to ceiling. As you look more closely at the pillars you realise they are in fact caryatids, depictions of women in full-length dresses with baskets on their heads, representing the fertility of the earth.

You realise the caryatids all have different contents carved in their baskets. The caryatid in the north-east has a basket full of flowers, the one in the south-east has sheaves of corn and other grains, the one on the south-west has apples, pears and other fruits, and the one in the north-west has hazelnuts and almonds and all different sorts of nuts within it.

CHAPTER 14

The Inner Talisman

Rather than making talismans which require you to either wear, carry or store them, you can effectively make yourself the talisman to attract the type of energy you are seeking to increase in your life (e.g. prosperity, health, etc).

The process is a simple one, which involves writing the intent on the charm (Earth), and then speaking the words of intent and blowing on the charm (Air). Once this is done you burn the charm (Fire), dropping the ashes into the water (Water), and consume the water taking the charm into yourself having released the intent into the universe. You are then the focus for the intent, having made it part of your being, and will act as a magnet drawing the energy attracted by your intent to yourself.

Prior to the rite you should have created the design for the charm. When you do make the charm, we recommend chlorine-free paper or card and non-toxic inks (always check toxicity). As you will be burning it and consuming the ashes in water, it is good to keep it small. You should also have prepared your statement of intent which describes the purpose of the rite.

Remember that factors like elemental timing may also be figured into the rite to increase effectiveness. Likewise, whilst the rite can be performed as a simple stand alone ceremony, it can also be worked during rituals using other techniques like the elemental pyramids. This will serve to give the rite a large initial boost as the level of elemental energy being drawn into your actions will be significantly higher.

For this rite you will require:

- Charm design, prepared beforehand
- Statement of intent, prepared beforehand
- Paper and pens for creating charm
- Chalice or bowl of spring water (or living water)
- Red candle

Ritual Sequence

- Write the intent of the charm on it, and copy any symbols or glyphs that form part of the design.
- State the intent and then blow on the charm saying, *By the power of Ruach haQadosh, the breath of life, I give purpose and direction to this intent.* See your breath being a pure lavender colour, and be aware of the charm becoming heavier as the intent settles into it.
- Set light to the charm over the fire candle. Say, *I declare my intent to the universe, that [statement of intent].* Feel the silence and stillness in the temple as your intent radiates outwards into the subtle realms.
- Hold it over the chalice of water (or bowl) and ensure the ashes all fall into the water.
- Drink the water with ashes in, saying, *I am the focus, as above, so below.* Feel the intent filling your body, permeating every cell, charging it and making you feel vibrant and joyful.

CHAPTER 15

Invocation of the Archangels

The following invocation is drawn from the seventeenth century *Nine Celestial Keys* of Dr Thomas Rudd (Sloane MS 3825 and Harley MS 6482). The material is unique in its manner of summoning the archangels directly to visible appearance, which does not occur in this manner in other Grimoires. The invocation is for Michael, but it can be used for the other elemental archangels by simply substituting the appropriate names as indicated in the table below. Note that in the original the invocation for Uriel is given as the same as Michael. As these are completely different angels, we have given the Venusian attributions here as we use them, which were attributed to Hanael in the original MSS, for consistency.

If you wish to make a lamen to wear, which is always a good idea for conjurations, the seals from Harley MS 6482, which use the angelic seals from the *Heptameron*, are recommended (though you would need to adapt the one for Michael to use for Uriel). The seals from Sloane MS 3825 make an excellent pentacle to use as the base for the crystal during the conjuration. Use the left hand side image as the top side of the pentacle, on which you place the crystal during the ceremony.

The initial invocation should be spoken with a strong insistent voice. The replication is used if you have had no response within fifteen minutes, and may be used up to three times in the subsequent time period. If for any reason you have still had no response after that, then perform a license to depart (see appendix 9) and open your circle. Remember that if you are calling an archangel to visible appearance in a crystal and to communicate with you, it is a sensible move to have your questions ready. You do not want to freeze and find yourself unable to think of what to say, this might not go down very well at all!

Archangel	Raphael	Michael	Gabriel	Uriel
Honoured Angel	Tetra	Salamia	Orphaniel	Dagael
Order of Angels	Archangels	Virtues	Angels	Principalities
Heaven	Second	Fourth	First	Third
Sphere	Mercury	Sol	Luna	Venus
Divine Name	Elohim Tzavaot	Eloah	Shaddai	Jahveh Tzavaot
Numeral Attribute	Hod	Tiphereth	Yesod	Netzach
Great Name	Adonai	Phaa	Marinata	Shaddai

The following conjuration and replication is for the invocation of the archangel Michael.

Conjuration of Michael

O you Glorious, Great, Sacred, & Celestial Angel & blessed Intelligence, Who are Called, Michael ; and all others ye Celestial Angels, Servants of the most high, Omnipotent, Incomprehensible, Immense, Immortal & Eternal God of Hosts, the Only Creator of Heaven & Earth, & of all things whatsoever, both Celestial, Elemental, Animal, Vegetable, Mineral & Reptile or Insect, that Is Contained & Comprehended therein, & that Serve before the great, High & most Excellent, & honoured Angel, Salamia, As Ministering Angels, present always at Divine Commands, in the Order or Hierarchy of Angels, Called Virtues, & Residing in the fourth Heaven, & bearing Rule, office, & power in the Orb or sphere of the planet Called Sol: we the servants Also of the highest, reverently here present in his holy fear, Do Call upon you and humbly request & Earnestly Entreat you, & move you, to Visible Appearance, in by and through, this ineffable great Mighty, Signal, Sacred, & Divine name of the most high God, Eloha; & his numeral Attribute Tiphereth, who Sitteth in the imperial & highest heaven, before whom all hosts or Choir of Celestial Angels Incessantly Singeth, O Mapa:La:man Hallelujah; who Created the Heavens, & the Earth, & the seas, & separated the Light from the Darkness, in the first Day of the Week, & also Decreed & Constituted & Appointed you to govern the Said first Day: &c: And Established all aforesaid by the Seal of his Incomprehensible, Mighty, holy, & great name: Phaa: as the most high & only God of Heaven & lord of hosts: the maker of time, & by the Seal of your Creation, being the Mark or Character of holiness unto you, & by the Occult Mystery, & Secret Virtue, Efficacy & Influence thereof, Dignifying & Confirming you, in Orders & office, name, Nature, & Corporature: with Divine Celestial, Angelical, Immortal, Eternal, & Sublime Excellency, Glory power, purity, perfection, Goodness & Love: first unto the service of the most high God & his Divine Laws & Commands, & nextly unto the Charge, Care & Conduct, Counsel, Comfort, benefit, & Assistance of his Servants the sons of men, living on Earth, to instruct & guide them Into the Knowledge & way of truth, & all true physical & Metaphysical Sciences, Either Immediately from the holy Ghost: unto More Choice Vessels of honour, or Mediately by Divine grace & permission from your self or Selves, unto the sons of men, Servants of God, Dwelling on Earth, whensoever you shall be of them Invocated, Called forth, & thereby moved to Descend and Appear unto them by all Aforesaid, & by the great & Signal Virtue, power, Dignity, Excellency & Efficacy thereof, both immediately primary & Mediately Secondary, by respective mediums of Divine Light grace & mercy, as Ordinately Dependent & so thereby flowing, & Accordingly Diffusing by Several Emanations proper, a Symbolising power & Virtue, from the Superior to the Inferior, we Do humbly beseech, & Earnestly Request, & incessantly Entreat you, O you Magnificent, Benevolent & Sacred Angel or Blessed Intelligence, Michael: Governing in the fourth Heaven Mansion, Orb, or Sphere of the planet Called Sol, together with all others ye benevolent Sacred & Celestial Angels, or Intelligences, Ministers of truth, & true Science & Sapience, both Celestial & terrestrial, as Messengers of Spiritual light, & Mediums of Divine Grace, Located, ruling & Residing in the Order or Hierarchy & office Called Virtues; in the fourth Heaven, Orb, or Sphere of the planet Called Sol, from the Superior to the Inferior, in General & particular, jointly & severally, Every & Each one, by office Respectively &c: to gird up, & gather your selves together, & some one or more of you, as it shall please God, & by Divine permission, to Move & Descend from your Celestial Mansion or place of Residence, into this Crystal Stone or Glass Receptacle And therein to Appear Visibly, unto us; & we Do also entreat you would be favourably pleased, In & through the same, to transmit your true Angelical & Real presence, plainly unto the Sight of our Eyes, & your Voices unto our Ears, that we may Visibly See you, & Audibly hear you speak unto us; Or otherwise appear out of the Same, as it shall please God & you his Servants of Divine grace, & Messengers of Mercy, seemeth most Meet proper & pertinent or best befitting this Action, Appearance, or Occasion, or Matter, & to show plainly & Visibly unto us, a foregoing Sign or test of your Appearance, & we also yet further humbly beseech, Earnestly Entreat, Undeniably request, & move you, O you Benevolent Glorious Angel, or Blessed Intelligence, Michael: together with all Others ye Sacred & Celestial Angels, or Blessed Intelligences, from the Superior to the Inferior, in power, & office, Residing in the fourth Heaven, Mansion, Orb, or Sphere of the planet or Star Called Sol, & serving the Divine Decrees, Commands & Appointments of the Highest, in the Office & order of Virtues, in by &

through this Divine, Signal, Mighty & powerful name of your God Eloha, & his numeral Attribute Tiphereth: & the great Efficacy, Virtue, Excellency, power, prevalence & Superiority thereof, to gird up & gather your Selves together, Every & Each one, jointly & severally by it Self Respectively; & to Move & Descend from your Celestial Mansion, or place of Residence, Apparently Visible to the Sight of our Eyes, in this Crystal Stone or Glass Receptacle Standing here before us, as being set for that purpose, or Otherwise unto us, out of the same as it shall please God, & you his Servants of Divine Light, grace & mercy, Seemeth good & most meet & best befitting this Action; & also to show forth a preceding Sign of your Appearance, and to be friendly unto us, & by your Angelical Benevolence, Celestial Illumination, favourable Assistance, familiar Society, Mutual Correspondence, Verbal Converse, Continual Community, & Sacred Instructions, both now at this time present, & at all times, to instruct, & Readily Direct our more Weak, Depraved, Stupid, & Ignorant Intellect, judgements & Understandings, & to Conduct us by your Angelical Instincts and Archidoctions, into the Luminous pathway of truth, Leading unto, & giving Entrance into the ports, Cities & palaces of wisdom & true Science, and make us partakers of Undefiled Knowledge, Without whose Angelical guide & spiritual Conduct, blessed Assistance, & benevolent Advertisements, it is impossible for us or any Mortal on Earth to find, or Obtain, or to be Esteemed worthy of Entrance; into with testimony wherefore we humbly Entreat & move you, O you great Sacred, & Celestial Ministering Angel or Intelligence, Michael; & all others you president, & inferior Angels, servants of the most high God, Residing & officiating in the fourth heaven Mansion, Orb, or Sphere of the planet Sol, in the Order or Hierarchy of Angels Called Virtues; who all Obediently Serve, & Readily fulfil, his Omnipotent Decrees & Commandments, in his Divine Dispensations, & Appointments, According to your general & Respective offices, in by & through his ineffable, Imperial, Great Signal, & Divine name Eloha, & his numeral Attribute, Tiphereth, and the power Efficacy, & Virtue thereof, we Servants also of the same your God, & by the Strength & force of our faith, & hope in him, for Divine Assistance, Grace & Mercy herein; Do Earnestly request, powerfully invocate and Confidently Move you, & Call you forth to Visible Appearance, here before us, in this Crystal Stone or Glass Receptacle or Otherwise thereout here before us, as it Shall please God, is given unto you So to Do; & likewise to show Visibly Unto us, a foregoing Sign of your Appearance, O you Servant of Mercy: Michael, and all Others the Celestial Ministering Angels, & Mediums of Divine grace & Light, from the Superior to the Inferior, Residing serving & officiating In the Order of Virtues: Move (we say) & by the Superior power And permission, & in the name of the highest Descend, Appear, & Visibly show your Selves, jointly or Severally, & Respectively unto us, in this Crystal Stone or Glass Receptacle Standing here before us, or Otherwise out of the Same, as it shall please God to permit & Appoint you, & to show us a preceding Sign thereof, & by your Mediate Angelical Inspiration, Information or Chief teachings, to instruct, help, Aid & assist us, both at this time present, & at all Other times & places, whensoever & wheresoever, we shall Invocate move & Call you forth to Visible Appearance, & to our Assistance, in whatsoever truth or Subject Matter or things, Appertaining thereunto, in all wisdom & true Science both Celestial & terrestrial &c: that shall be necessary for us, & also as any Other Emergent Occasion, Shall Duly & properly Require, to the advancement & Setting forth of God's Glory, & the Improvement of our Welfare, Comfort, & benefit of our Worldly & temporal Estate & Condition, whilst we yet Live, likewise in Such matters or things whatsoever Else, that shall be Necessary for us to Know & Enjoy, Even beyond what we are able to ask or think, which the Almighty giver of all good gifts, shall in his bountiful & paternal mercy, be graciously pleased hereby to give you, to reveal & show forth unto us; Or, Otherwise to bestow upon us, O you great Angel or Blessed Intelligence Michael: And all Others ye Celestial Angels of the Order of Virtues, Mediums of Divine Grace, & Mercy, Ministers of true Light & Understanding, & Servants of the most

High God particularly Recited, & spoken of, invocated, Moved & Called forth, to Visible Appearance as aforesaid, Descend, (we say) & by the power of Superior Emission, Some one or more of you, Appear Visibly here before us, as it shall please God, & be friendly unto us, & in your Respective offices, Do for us as for the Servants of the most high God, whereunto we move you all, In power & presence, whose works shall be a song of honour & the praise of your God, in your Creation Amen.

Replication (Second Conjuration)

O ye Glorious Angel, or Blessed intelligence, who by name is Called Michael : And all Others the Sacred Celestial Angels, of the Order of Virtues, Residing & Located by Mansion proper, in that Orb, or sphere of Heaven Called the Sun: particularly Recited, Mentioned, Moved & Called forth, to Visible Appearance, as in the foregoing Invocation, is and hath been of us Lately, & more at Large Rehearsed, Earnestly Solicited, Supplicated & humbly Requested, by the Virtue power, force, & Efficacy whereof, & by all the Royal words & Sentences therein Contained, & also by the great Mighty powerful & Excellent name of the Most high God Eloha, & his numeral Attribute Tiphereth: Or otherwise, by the truest & most Especial name of your God, we the servants also of the highest, reverently here present in his holy fear, Attending his Divine grace, Mercy & good pleasure, paternally unto us herein, Do by the Strength & power, of our faith, hope, & Confidence in our God, & our Confirmation in his holy Spirit, Dignifying us, with Superior power & perfection, humbly Entreat, & Earnestly Request, & powerfully Move you, O you great Angels, or Blessed Intelligences, from the Superior to the Inferior, in general & particular, Every & Each one, for, and by it self Respectively, by Degrees, Nature & office, residing, & being in the Mansion or fourth Heaven, Orb or Sphere of the planet, or Star Called the Sun: & Serving the Commands of the highest, in the Order or Hierarchy of Angels, Called Virtues: Move Therefore O ye great & glorious Angel,

Michael; or Some One or More, or Either of you, O ye sacred Celestial Angels, of the Order of Virtues, by Degree, nature & office, & by the Virtue, power, & Efficacy of all aforesaid, Descend & appear Visibly, here before us, & unto us, in this Crystal Stone or Glass Receptacle or Otherwise, out of the same, here before us as it shall please God: & also, you his Messengers of Divine grace, & Mercy, & to show forth plainly unto us, Some Remarkable Sign or token, foregoing your Coming & appearance, & to be friendly unto us, & Do for us, as for the Servants of the Highest, Whereunto in his name, we Do, again Earnestly request, & Move you, both, in power & presence, whose friendship unto us herein, & works shall be a song of honour, & the praise of your God in your Creation: Amen.

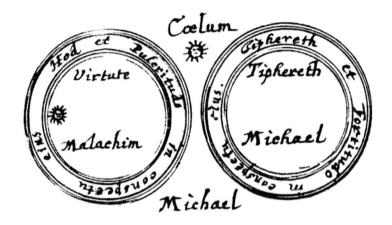

Seal of Michael from Sloane MS 3825 f. 75v

Seal of Michael from Harley MS 6482 f. 241v

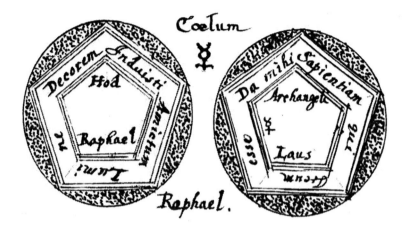

Seal of Raphael from Sloane MS 3825 f. 86

Seal of Raphael from Harley MS 6482 f. 265

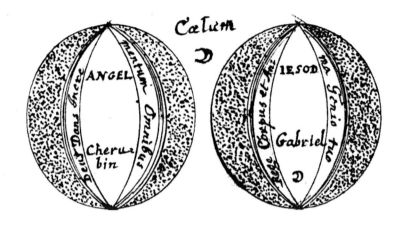

Seal of Gabriel from Sloane MS 3825 f. 91

Seal of Gabriel from Harley MS 6482 f. 277v

CHAPTER 16

Elementaries

The idea of creating thought forms using elemental energy is a common one in the modern Western Esoteric Traditions, and one which is sometimes referred to by the term Elementary (and also by other terms like servitor). In his classic work *Magic: White and Black*, the German magician Franz Hartmann gives a lucid description of the elementary, calling it an elemental form.

"Elemental forms being the servants of their creator – in fact, his own self – may be used by him for good or evil purposes. Loves and hates may create subjective forms of beautiful or of horrid shapes, and, being infused with consciousness, obtain life, and may be sent on some errand for good or for evil."[46]

Confusingly, Paracelsus also used the term elementary to refer to the astral shell of a dead person, left behind after death when the soul departs. This shell may retain aspects of the personality and was said to often masquerade as an elemental, hence the term elementary. This term has been frequently used in this manner in Theosophy, popularised in the writings of figures like Madame Blavatsky. Paracelsus also used the term *aquastor* to describe a being created by

---

46 Magic: White and Black, Hartmann, 1888.

the power of the imagination, which is what we today would understand by the term elementary.

So to be clear, we refer to an elementary as a being formed from elemental force and formulated by the imagination and will of the practitioner(s). Elementaries are created for a whole range of purposes, and are usually created from a single element or all four. There is no set rule to this, it depends entirely on the purpose that the elementary is created for. Their purpose is to carry out a set task determined by the practitioner(s). Elementaries can be created to accomplish any manner of task, and may have any form, but the form should be sympathetic to the task, and the task of realistic proportion.

When this type of elementary is created it should be named and given a lifespan, dissolving back into its constituent elements at the end of its lifespan. General tasks should not be set, precision is required in creating an elementary and setting its task, e.g. heal X of condition Y within a specified time. As with burned sigils, elementaries should be forgotten about after creation. The elementary should be given the necessary skills to achieve its task, e.g. ability to locate a specified person, ability to heal, etc, and these abilities should be named during the creation. Remember the KISS principle when creating Elementaries (Keep It Simple Stupid).

If an elementary is to have a long life span (beyond a few lunar months), it may be attached to a physical object, such as a crystal, talisman, statue, etc or housed in a spirit bottle or jar. This is particularly relevant for an elementary that is created as a guardian for a house or temple, for which fire is commonly used in the creation. Conversely the object should be small and portable if it is likely to be moved around, such as for a guardian for a vehicle, or a person. In the latter case the classic idea of attaching the guardian to a piece of jewellery can be applied to good effect, and air, which travels well, is more effective for the basis of the elementary.

Air is also good for creating elementaries for intellectual work, such as studying, and also for help in passing exams. Earth is particularly good for issues relating to prosperity and stability. You should be aware that elementaries are useful magickal creations, but not become dependent on them. With this in mind we should mention two specific areas which can easily generate problems, even with consideration. These are emotional issues and healing.

Creating an elementary to deal with an emotional issue is asking for trouble. Emotions do not do well when taken absolutely literally, which is what an elementary will do. This means one issue will be exaggerated out of proportion to any others, which may lead to obsession. Likewise history does indicate that watery elemental beings and emotions do not really mix very well, and are the most likely recipe for disaster.

When it comes to healing you need to be phenomenally careful. In fact it is more a case of, if in doubt, leave it out! You need to consider carefully the nature of the health problem, and then decide which element(s) will work to combat it. What you must avoid is using an element that is going to make the condition worse. Thus if someone had a breathing problem, you might think, aha, I will use air to form my elementary, which would be completely wrong. Air would just help feed and spread the condition, and what you would actually need would be earth, the opposite of air, to stabilise and give form to the condition so it can be stopped and more easily located and dealt with. Consult chapter 3 *The Interaction of the Four Elements*, before you attempt to make a healing elementary.

Creation of an Elementary

Preparation

The exact form, lifespan, name, skills and task should have already been determined precisely. Likewise a mantra of the abilities should already have been prepared. The practitioner(s) should sit (in a circle if more than one) and will visualise it in the centre of the magick circle. The direction the elementary is facing should also have been predetermined, so that if there is more than one practitioner they see the appropriate view (side, front, back).

Execution

- Create the magick circle as preferred.
- Call spiritual creatures as preferred (or not).
- Use a technique to fill the magick circle with an appropriate form of elemental energy for the creation of the elementary, such as vibrating divine names, the appropriate pyramid, etc.
- Visualise the elementary and name it, stating its lifespan, qualities and purpose. E.g. *"I name you Venbu, and form you from the element of Air, giving you a lifespan of a week. You will have the qualities of clear-headedness and vigour, and will assist [Name] by strengthening these qualities in her so she will pass her exam."*
- The practitioner(s) should then chant the mantra of the elementary's powers whilst fixing its form through visualisation. Additionally the elemental energy in the magick circle is focused into the elementary to give it the energy it needs to complete its task.
- The order is then given to the elementary, re-stating its task clearly and concisely. E.g. *"Venbu, you will go forth, find*

[Name] and give her the energy and clear-headedness she needs to pass her exam. You have one week to perform this task, after which you will return to the element from which you came."

- As you give the order, you should visualise the desired result, so it can be sent as a signal to the elementary to ensure it understands the task it has been set.
- Open your magick circle and write up in your magickal diary.

CHAPTER 17

The Elemental Deities

"Now hear the fourfold Roots of everything:
Enlivening Hera, Aidoneus, bright Zeus,
And Nestis, moistening mortal springs with tears."[47]

With this verse Empedocles introduced the concept that the elements were in fact manifestations of divine power. This is the source of the attribution of air and fire as masculine elements, stemming from Zeus and Hades (Aidoneus), and earth and water as feminine elements, stemming from Hera and Persephone (Nestis). Empedocles taught by allegory and poetic allusion, and so there has been some dispute about the attributions of the gods to the elements. This is convincingly solved by Peter Kingsley in his work *Ancient Philosophy, Mystery, and Magic.*

Decades later the Greek philosopher Philolaos attributed the elements only to male gods, attributing air to Dionysus, fire to Ares, earth to Hades and water to Chronos.

Of course when we consider the four elements in the Greek pantheon, other deities also spring to mind, and we will also consider these where relevant. Although they were not attributed as an elemental grouping, it is worth mentioning gods from the earlier

---

47 Tetrasomia, Empedocles, C5th BCE.

pantheons which have contributed to the Western Mystery Tradition, i.e. Egypt and Sumeria.

	Sumeria	Egypt	Greece
Air	Enlil Ninlil	Amun Shu	Aeolus Anemoi Zeus
Earth	Ninhursag	Geb	Gaia Hera
Fire	Utu	Re Sekhmet	Hades Hephaistos
Water	Enki	Neith Nun	Persephone Poseidon

However, having considered other gods, let us return to the attributions made by Empedocles. This was made in the form of a riddle, as was much of his teaching. However when we look at his attributions we can see the symmetry in his logic. Zeus, the air god is wed to Hera the earth goddess, the opposite element, symbolising the marriage of heaven and earth.

Likewise Hades the fire god is wed to Persephone the water goddess, again the opposite element, and in this case symbolising the marriage of transformation.

The Air Gods

Zeus is a storm god, with his thunderbolts, exemplifying the power of air as the medium of change. Zeus also shape-shifted on many occasions, another airy trait, though usually it was to seduce a goddess, nymph or woman. The reference by Empedocles to Zeus as *bright* refers to the view of the Mediterranean sky as bright, the vivid sky blue which could dazzle the unwary. Empedocles also referred to Zeus as *'cloud-gatherer'*, a rather large hint as to the attribution he had in mind.

Aeolus (*'Sparkling'*), the wind god, ruled the Anemoi (*'Wind Gods'*, called *Venti* by the Romans). These are commonly known as Euros, Notus, Zephyrus and Boreas, being the children of the dawn goddess Eos (*'Dawn'*) and the stellar god Astraios (*'Starry'*). Originally there were three Anemoi – Notus, Boreas and Zephyrus. Each one of these gods was connected with one of the ancient Greek Seasons (they had three not four) and then Euros was later added for Autumn. Boreas is the purple-winged god of Winter, Zephyrus is the god of spring and Notus is the storm-bringing god of wet weather corresponding to late Summer and Autumn. These gods of the winds show that the modern correspondences between seasons, elements and directions are not all the same now as they were in the past. It should also be observed that they are all wind gods, and so traditions where they are called on to represent the elements are being inaccurate in their usage.

Wind	Meaning	Season
Euros (Eurus)	East Wind	Autumn
Notus (Auster)	South Wind	Summer
Zephyrus (Favonius)	West Wind	Spring
Boreas (Aquilo)	North Wind	Winter

Hymn to Zeus

O Father Zeus, who shakes with fiery light
The world deep-sounding from thy lofty height:
Thy power divine, the flaming lightning shrouds,
With dark investiture, in fluid rolling clouds.
With roaring flames involving all around,
And bolts of thunder of tremendous sound.
Sudden, unconquered, holy, thundering God,
With noise unbounded, flying all abroad;
Thy thunders white, the azure garments tear,
And burst the veil of all surrounding air.
Propitious to these sacred rites incline,
And crown my wishes with a life divine:
Add royal health, and gentle peace beside,
With equal reason, for my constant guide.

The Fire Gods

Hades rules Tartaros, the fiery realm. Empedocles, living in the shadow of Mount Etna, was very aware of the fire in the earth, as seen in his writings, where he commented, *"There are many fires burning beneath the surface of the earth."* It is interesting that he should have effectively predicted the molten core of the earth, which is liquid fire, or the marriage of Hades and Persephone. Subsequent religions would also draw from this idea, giving us the Hebrew Gehenna, a fiery hell, which would also be mirrored in the later Christian view of hell.

Empedocles referred to Hades as destructive fire (the fire of death in the underworld), and on two occasions referred to the smith god Hephaistos as representing positive fire, the fire used by the master craftsman. From studying his writings it is clear he viewed them as two sides of the same god – both living underground (Hephaistos lived under Mount Etna) in the fire.

Hymn to Hades

Hades, magnanimous, whose realms profound
Are fixed beneath the firm and solid ground,
In the Tartarian plains remote from sight,
And wrapt forever in the depths of night;
Earth's keys to thee, illustrious king belong,
Its secret gates unlocking, deep and strong.
The flames that burn within the earth's great heart
The fiery roots are thine alone to impart
O mighty dæmon, whose decision dread,
The future fate determines of the dead,
O power all-ruling, holy, honoured light,
Thee sacred poets and their hymns delight:
Propitious to thy mystic's works incline,
Rejoicing come, for holy rites are thine.

The Water Gods

Nestis was a local Sicilian name for the goddess Persephone. Empedocles was Sicilian, and was undoubtedly influenced by his landscape. This included the active volcano Mount Etna, and also the temple to Hekate, Demeter and Persephone, with its sacred spring to Persephone. Springs, wells and other water sources into the earth were particularly sacred to Persephone, and were seen as entrances to the underworld. This is a viewpoint that would also be found in the Celtic worldview. Persephone was also associated with the milk of immortality, which sprang from her breasts, as seen in references such as *"I have made straight for the Breast of the Mistress, the Queen of the Underworld."*[48] She thus represented both the life-giving and destructive aspects of water.

Poseidon, the mighty sea god who was also the god of earthquakes, is another watery deity. When the Olympian gods defeated Chronos, Poseidon was given the sea as his realm, which he ruled with his brazen trident. Poseidon was also the god of rivers, and of flood and drought, who caused more than one river to dry up when the local river god annoyed him.

---

48 Gold Tablet Zuntz A1-3, C5th BCE.

Hymn to Persephone

Daughter of Zeus, almighty and divine,
Come, blessed queen, and to these rites incline:
Only-begotten, Hades' honoured wife,
O venerable Goddess, source of life:
Jove's holy offspring, of a beauteous mien,
Fatal, with lovely locks, infernal queen:
Illustrious, horned, of a bounteous mind,
Alone desired by those of mortal kind.
Espoused in Autumn: life and death alone
To wretched mortals from thy power is known:
For thine the task according to thy will,
Life to produce, and all that lives to kill.
Send Health with gentle hand, and crown my life
With blest abundance, free from noisy strife.

The Earth Gods

Hera may seem a strange choice to be the goddess of elemental Earth. However it should be remembered that one of the primary qualities of earth is stability, and Hera was the protectress of the stability of family life. Empedocles described Hera as *'enlivening'* or *'life-bringing'*, an epithet used for goddesses associated with the earth, specifically Gaia and Demeter.

Gaia was the original goddess of the earth, the primal goddess who gave birth to the Titans and numerous other gods, demi-gods, monsters and daimones over the centuries. She represents the whole earth, and has been popularised in recent years by the Gaia hypothesis, that the earth with all its life-forms is a single self-regulating organism.

Hymn to Hera

O Royal Hera of majestic mien,
Divinely formed, divine, Zeus' blessed queen,
Throned in the bosom of cærulean air,
The race of mortals is thy constant care.
Thy wondrous enlivening power inspires,
To nourish growth, which every life desires.
Mother of families and homes, from thee alone
Producing all things, mortal life is known:
All natures share thy temperament divine,
And universal sway alone is thine.
With founding blasts of wind, the swelling sea
And rolling rivers roar, when shook by thee.
Come, blessed Goddess, famed almighty queen,
With aspect kind, rejoicing and serene.

APPENDIX

APPENDIX 1

Four or Three plus One?

"That, then, from which the whole Cosmos is formed, consisteth of Four Elements – Fire, Water, Earth, and Air; Cosmos itself is one, its Soul is one, and God is one."[49]

Although the elements are grouped as a quaternary, they also occur as a combination of three plus one. The division could be described as based on movement and form, as the one is the static and solid earth, and the triad is air, fire, water, the mobile and fluid elements. The division is seen clearly in the Qabalistic attributions, where air, fire and water are attributed to the three Hebrew mother letters of Aleph (A), Shin (Sh) and Mem (M).

Aleph is the divine breath as *"the Spirit of God hovered over the face of the waters."*[50] The waters are Mem, the second mother letter. The third letter, Shin [fire] is implied by the next line (as light is an aspect of fire), *"And God said: 'Let there be light' and there was light."*[51]

This is expressed differently in the *Sepher Yetzirah*, where it describes the creation:

---

49 The Perfect Sermon, Thrice-Greatest Hermes, Mead (ed).

50 Genesis 1:2.

51 Genesis 1:3.

"Three Mothers, AMSh, in the Universe are air, water, fire.
Heaven was created from fire
Earth was created from water
And air from Breath decides between them."[52]

This division of three plus one is also seen in the division of the realms by the Greek gods, with the three divine brothers effectively dividing the elements. Zeus rules heaven (air), Poseidon rules the sea (water) and Hades rules Tartaros (fire). The earth is held in common between them.

The three plus one elements motif are also seen in a version of the Greek tale of the creation of mankind, though with fire as the single element. Prometheus formed man from earth and water and Athena breathed air into him, but it was not until Prometheus stole fire and gave it to man that he was complete.

Interestingly a threefold division is also seen in relation to the Greek goddess Hekate. Zeus bestows upon Hekate *"a share of the earth and the unfruitful sea. She received honour also in starry heaven."*[53] So Hekate has the threefold attributes of earth, water (sea) and air (starry heaven), which leaves the fourth element of fire as evident in her nature as Phosphorus (light-bringer), bearing the twin torches. The elemental connection to Hekate may also be seen tangentially in the fact that Empedocles, the creator of the doctrine of the four elements, was probably a priest of Hekate.[54] Hekate's connection to the four elements as a whole was emphasised in the sixth century by John Lydus in his work *Liber De Mensibus*.

---

52 Sepher Yetzirah 3:4, C3rd CE.

53 Theogony, Hesiod, C8th-7th BCE.

54 See Ancient Philosophy, Mystery and Magic; Empedocles and the Pythagorean Tradition, Kingsley, 1995 for a detailed explanation of this.

"From whence they [the Chaldean tradition] hand down the mystical doctrine concerning the four elements and four-headed Hekate. For the fire-breathing head of a horse is clearly raised towards the sphere of fire, and the head of a bull, which snorts like some bellowing spirit, is raised towards the sphere of air; and the head of a hydra as being of a sharp and unstable nature is raised towards the sphere of water, and that of a dog as having a punishing and avenging nature is raised towards the sphere of earth."[55]

The three elements are seen in alchemy, with salt (earth), mercury (water) and sulphur (fire) being the triad which are required to produce the azoth (air). Here the intangible and elusive goal, is the one which is actually present in one form all the time – a good allegory for the practice of magick, in fact!

---

55 De Mensibus, Wunsch (ed), 1898.

APPENDIX 2

Symbols of the Four Elements

The best know elemental symbols are the set of triangles formed from the hexagram. The hexagram represents the universe, and the formation of the four elemental triangles from this figure demonstrates the concept of the elements as the building blocks of physicality.

Air and Fire are both represented by an upward pointing triangle, which represents their expansive (warm) nature. The upward triangle also symbolises the male phallus. The bar on the air triangle demonstrates that it is a denser element than fire.

Water and Earth are both represented by a downward pointing triangle, which represents their contractive (cool) nature. The downward triangle symbolises the female pubic triangle (i.e. genitalia). The bar on the earth triangle demonstrates that it is a denser element than water.

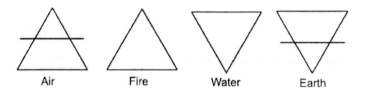

Air   Fire   Water   Earth

APPENDIX 3

Elemental Fragrances

When burning elemental fragrances, pure resins may be used to good effect, or mixed incense created for the same purpose. For convenience we include here a list of common resins and herbs with their elemental attributions.

Element	Fragrance
Air	Copal, Elemi, Fennel ,Galbanum, Labdanum, Lavender, Mastic, Sage, Tolu Balsam
Fire	Amber, Bay, Cinnamon, Clove, Dragon's Blood, Frankincense, Ginger, Juniper, Opoponax, Saunderswood (Red Sandlewood)
Water	Ambergris, Camphor, Cypress, Dammar, Hyssop, Jasmine, Lotus, Peru Balsam, Ylang Ylang
Earth	Aloes, Benzoin, Cedar, Colophony (Pine Resin), Myrrh, Patchouli, Rose, Sandalwood, Spikenard, Storax, Vetivert

APPENDIX 4

The Elements and Minerals

Agrippa gives a description of specific minerals and types associated with the four elements in his *Three Books of Occult Philosophy.*

"For amongst the stones they especially are called earthy that are dark, and more heavy; and those waterish, which are transparent, and are compacted of water, as crystal, beryl, and pearls in the shells of fishes: and they are called airy, which swim upon the water, and are spongious, as the stones of a sponge, the pumice stone, and the stone sophus:[56] *and they are called fiery, out of which fire is extracted, or which are resolved into fire, or which are produced of fire: as thunderbolts, firestones, and the stone asbestos. Also amongst metals, lead and silver are earthy: quicksilver is waterish: copper, and tin are airy: and gold, and iron are fiery."*[57]

From a practical perspective, many associations have developed since Agrippa, and we present a rationalised list of the most common and coherent ones for use in elemental magick. Some of these disagree with Agrippa's attributions given in the quote above, but the ones we have given are consistent with the planetary attributions, which is often not the case for Agrippa.

---

56 Sophus, or tophus, is a general name for porous stones produced as sediments or incrustations.

57 Three Books of Occult Philosophy, Agrippa.

These correspondences may be utilised in various ways, such as for amulets or talismans, foci for workings, or simply as a magnet to attract more of the appropriate elemental energy to you on an ongoing basis.

Element	Air	Fire	Water	Earth
Precious	Topaz	Ruby	Sapphire	Emerald
Semi-Precious	Agate Amethyst Azurite Citrine Quartz Labradorite Lapis Lazuli Sodalite Turquoise	Carnelian Cat's Eye Garnet Heliotrope Hematite Magnetite Pyrites Spinel Sunstone Tigers Eye	Aquamarine Beryl Chalcedony Gypsum Moonstone Quartz Selenite	Amazonite Jadeite Malachite Nephrite Onyx Peridot Rose Quartz Serpentine Smoky Quartz Zoisite
Non-Crystal	Opal	Amber Obsidian	Abalone Coral Ivory Pearl	Jet
Metal	Mercury Tin	Gold Iron (Brass)[58]	Silver	Copper Lead

---

58 Although brass is an alloy, it is often referred to in magickal texts, hence its inclusion here.

The Elements and Plants

Plants have long been associated with individual elements, and this is particularly found in the work of Empedocles and the root magicians of ancient Greece. These ideas were further developed by Paracelsus in the sixteenth century with his *Doctrine of Signatures*, which based attributions of plants on colour and appearance.

	Plant
Air	Agrimony, Alfalfa, Alkanet, Arnica, Bayberry, Betony, Borage, Caraway, Cedar, Chervil, Cinquefoil, Copal, Dill, Dock, Eucalyptus, Fumitory, Herb Mercury, Hyssop, Lavender, Lemon, Lime, Liquorice, Mace, Maple, Marjoram, Mastic, Moly, Poplar, Saffron, Sage, Sandalwood, Shamrock, St Johns Wort, Storax, Tragacanth, Vervain
Fire	Acacia, Angelica, Ash (Tree), Balsam, Basil, Bay, Black Pepper, Butterbur, Buttercup, Calamus, Capsicum, Chamomile, Celandine, Centaury, Chilli, Cinnamon, Dragons Blood, Eyebright, Frankincense, Galangal, Gentian, Ginger, Gorse, Heliotrope, Hickory, Hyacinth, Juniper, Marigold, Mistletoe, Mustard, Nettle, Oak, Opoponax, Orange, Orris, Palm, Peony, Pepper, Pine, Saffron, St Johns Wort, Storax, Sunflower, Thistle, Tobacco, Vine, Walnut
Water	Adders Tongue, Alder, Aniseed, Artemisia, Camphor, Cleavers, Hazel, Honeysuckle, Iris, Jasmine, Jojoba, Lignum Aloes, Lily, Mangrove, Moonwort, Mugwort, Poppy, Ranunculus, Saxifrage, Thyme, Turmeric, Watercress, Willow, Wintergreen, Witchazel, Ylang Ylang
Earth	Aconite, Adam & Eve Root, Asafoetida, Balm, Belladonna, Benzoin, Bergamot, Civet, Clover, Cypress, Daffodil, Datura, Elder, Geranium, Hellebore, Hemlock, Henbane, Lady's Mantle, Lilac, Myrrh, Myrtle, Pennyroyal, Peppermint, Primrose, Rose, Saunderswood, Sulphur, Sycamore, Venus Fly Trap, Violet, Yew

APPENDIX 6

The Elements and Animals

The best known animal associations with the elements are those of the four kerubic creatures, associated with the order of angels called the Kerubim (*'the Strong Ones'*). These angels have four heads and three sets of wings, and the four heads have become viewed as symbolising the elemental associations. There is sometimes confusion with these attributions as they are also attributed to the fixed signs of the zodiac, and do not seem to fit exactly, having been changed in the nineteenth century.

Leo as the lion and Taurus as the bull need no further consideration. However it was the switching of the eagle and man which has caused confusion. In the Grimoires and pre-nineteenth century texts the eagle is (logically) attributed to the element of Air, and hence to the zodiacal sign of Aquarius. Man, as the emotional creature, was attributed to the element of Water and the zodiacal sign of Scorpio. This was changed by some magicians in the nineteenth century as can be seen in the Golden Dawn and often subsequently, to man being attributed to Aquarius, and the eagle-snake-scorpion triplicity to Scorpio. We use the traditional associations as we feel they are more appropriate and logical, but it is up to use which you prefer based on how they feel in your practice and instincts.

Element	Air	Fire	Water	Earth
Sign	Aquarius	Leo	Scorpio	Taurus
Animal	Eagle	Lion	Man	Bull
Revised	Man	Lion	Eagle	Bull

These associations aside, there are other attributions which are both obvious and less obvious. The categories from the Grimoires are flying (air), crawling (fire), swimming (water) and creeping (earth).

APPENDIX 7

Names of Power

Various systems and sources give names of power associated with the elements, so we have gathered the most common ones here for convenience. If a set works for you, then include it in your workings where appropriate.

	Air	Earth	Fire	Water
Almadel	Adonaij, Helomi, Pine	Tetragrammaton, Shaddai, Jah	Helion, Heloi, Heli	Jod, Hod, Agla
7th Book of Moses	Jehovah, Shaddai, Eloha, Adonai	Athatos, Elion, Adonai, Tzavaot	Eheieh, Ihiros, Agla, Aysh, Jehovah	Tetragrammaton, Alpha et Omega, Adonai
Qabalah	Jah, Jahveh, Jahveh Tzavaot	Jahveh Tzabaot, Elohim Tzabaot	Elohim Gibor, Eloha, Eloah vaDaath	El, Shaddai, Shaddai El Chi
Enochian	Oro Ibah Aozpi	Emor Dial Hectega	Oip Teaa Pedoce	Empeh Arsol Gaiol
GD	Jahveh	Agla	Adonai	Eheih

Intonation of Words of Power

Reference is made throughout this work to the intonation (i.e. vibration) of divine names and words of power. This is an extremely powerful and yet also very simple technique to master and use in your magickal work.

To vibrate a word you need to breathe from your diaphragm, and prolong the duration of the syllables. Do not use shallow breaths, which is the norm for most people. You will soon know when you have found the right pitch for your vibrations, as you will literally feel your rib-cage, and possibly the rest of your body, vibrate with the power of the word you are uttering.

Vibrating a name does not mean that you have to shout or be very loud; the important thing is to find the right pitch for you which causes an internal vibration. This pitch varies from person to person, and requires no musical knowledge or ability. Once you have found this pitch, there are two more stages to the vibratory formula. These are the use of colour, and the optional visualization of the name.

For the colour, when you inhale to pronounce the words, visualise the air in front of you in its appropriate elemental colour. When you inhale, feel the energy entering your body and suffusing your being with its power. See your aura being tinged with the elemental colour, showing the spread of elemental power through your entire being.

The second (optional) stage is to visualise the name in the air in flaming letters of the appropriate colour. When you inhale you can draw the power of the name into yourself, or alternatively if you are using it as a ward, when you exhale you can breathe power into the name to further reinforce it. This works best with magickal languages such as Hebrew (remember Hebrew is written right to left), or Greek, but if you find this too difficult visualise the name in the Roman letters normally used for the English alphabet.

By breathing properly and vibrating words, and focusing your mind through the use of the correct colours, you will notice it is easier to achieve altered states of consciousness. You will be more aware of both the energy you generate, and also the energies around you.

Vibration Exercise

Try with the Tetragrammaton as Yah-veh (IHVH), seeing the name and the air you inhale as a pure soft blue. Practice until you can feel your body vibrating as you intone the syllables, drawing them out so that each of the two syllables takes 5-10 seconds to vibrate.

APPENDIX 9

License to Depart

The License to Depart is a standard part of the Grimoire tradition, releasing any summoned spiritual creatures to return to their own realm. However, more than this, it is important as it also releases any spiritual creatures which have, whether intentionally or unintentionally, been drawn to your magickal work. It is important to note that the License is a command rather than an instruction. You are not asking the spiritual creature to leave – you are telling it to leave. You need to be sure that the temple or magick circle is secure for you to leave and not encounter any negative or adverse effects from mischievous or malicious beings. Sadly the License has often been neglected by modern magickal traditions, which is something that hopefully will change. When you speak the License, see the air that you exhale with the words charged with a brilliant gold light, which fills the whole temple.

The License

I give license to depart to all spiritual creatures here present, in the mighty and holy names of Eheia and Agla, return to your realm immediately, not returning until you are summoned again; go with my blessings, and let there be peace eternally between you and me, in the mighty and holy names of Jahveh and Adonai.

APPENDIX 10

The Pentagram

The pentagram has become synonymous with the practice of magick. This symbol has been used almost universally throughout history, and as a result has a huge amount of power in it. This has resulted in its use as a very effective protection and ward.

The Sumerians were using the pentagram by 3000 BCE, often drawing it inverted. They called it *Ub*, meaning *'region'*, *'direction'* or *'heavenly quarter'*. The Sumerians used a five direction system of East, South, West, North and Above, with Above corresponding to the goddess Inanna, so it has been speculated that these directions were attributed by them to the pentagram, giving the original directional attributions on the pentagram.

In ancient Greece, the Pythagoreans called the pentagram Ugieia, meaning *'soundness'*. They wrote the letters of this word around the points of the pentagram, getting round the extra letter in the word by combining the epsilon (e) and second iota (i) to make a theta (th) which looks the same as the two vowels combined. They thus labelled the points of the pentagram with the letters upsilon (U), gamma (G), iota (I), theta (Th), and alpha (A). This was effectively an acronym, as these also gave the first letters of words corresponding to the elements.

Thus we have *Hudor* (Water),[59] *Gaia* (Earth), *Hierion* (divine or holy thing, i.e. Spirit),[60] *Therma* (Heat i.e. Fire) and *Aer* (Air) corresponding to the points of the pentagram.

These attributions started at the top and went anticlockwise around the pentagram, giving a very different set of attributions to those used in magickal traditions today. Comparing them we see:

Point	Greek	GD/Wicca
Top	Water	Spirit
Upper left	Earth	Air
Lower left	Spirit	Earth
Lower right	Fire	Fire
Upper right	Air	Water

(Contemporary attributions of the elements to the pentagram)

---

59 The H is added to the beginning of the word in transliteration from the Greek, so it actually starts with the letter U (upsilon).

60 Again the H is added in transliteration, so the word starts with the letter I (iota).

The Greek letters can be seen drawn around an inverse pentagram in Agrippa's *Three Books of Occult Philosophy*, showing that this idea was recognised and used in the sixteenth century.

The attributions may have changed from the ancient Greek ones to those used in modern magick with the Elizabethan magus Dr John Dee. The Great Table of Dee's Enochian system is comprised of the Four Elemental Tablets combined. The sequence of their combination is relevant for the elemental attributions, as the elemental attributions applied to the pentagram were clearly derived from here.

When creating the Great Table, the top half (or row) is formed by placing the Tablet of Air on the left and the Tablet of Water on the right, as you look at it. Likewise the bottom half (or row) is formed by placing the Tablet of Earth on the left and the Tablet of Fire on the right. If you then read anticlockwise from Air in the top left, the sequence is alphabetical, proceeding to Earth in the bottom left, Fire in the bottom right and Water in the top right, exactly as is seen with the elemental attributions on the points of the pentagram (with Spirit at the top).

Invoking Elemental Pentagrams

Banishing Elemental Pentagrams

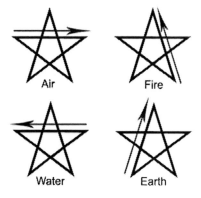

APPENDIX 11

Other Systems of Elements

The best known other system of elements is probably the Chinese one. This has five elements as opposed to four, and replaces air with wood and metal. Thus it comprises fire, water, earth, wood and metal. The Chinese system is not easily compatible with the western attributions, and so we include it here for the sake of interest. The Chinese elements are attributed thus:

Element	Colour	Season	Direction
Wood	Green	Spring	East
Fire	Red	Summer	South
Earth	Yellow	-	Centre
Metal	White	Autumn	West
Water	Black	Winter	North

The Indian system of the elements started with three elements of fire, water and earth, which equated to the three gunas or principles (and which are equated to the three alchemical principles). Later the elements of air and akasha (aether or spirit) were added, making it akin to the Western system.

Element	Colour	Guna	Principle	Tendency
Fire	Red	Rajas	Energy	Creation
Water	White	Sattva	Essence	Preservation
Earth	Black	Tamas	Mass	Destruction

Another well known elemental system is the Norse. This is more akin to the Western magickal system, having the same four elements of air, fire, water and earth, however it also includes ice as an element. The Norse culture being based in lands which knew ice very well, it is no surprise that ice should play such a significant role in their creation myth and elemental system, even having a rune named after it (Isa – meaning Ice).

APPENDIX 12

Elements in the Zodiac

The elements manifest through the zodiac in three elemental sets, these being cardinal, fixed and mutable. Each set has a particular type of behaviour which consequently affects the elements within it. Thus the cardinal elements are activating signs, initiating action and acting as a source of energy. The fixed signs are persistent signs, though resistant to change. The mutable signs are adaptable, and act as a bridge between the cardinal and fixed signs.

The elemental qualities in relation to the stars and the zodiac would form a complete book by itself, and it is not our intention to go into detail here. We simply draw attention to the fact that the elements relate to the zodiac, and in this permutation to the process of alchemical change through the twelve steps sometimes seen in the alchemical transformation.

Sign	Element	Type	Ruler	Zodiacal Man
Aries	Fire	Cardinal	Mars	Head
Taurus	Earth	Fixed	Venus	Throat
Gemini	Air	Mutable	Mercury	Arms
Cancer	Water	Cardinal	Moon	Chest
Leo	Fire	Fixed	Sun	Heart
Virgo	Earth	Mutable	Mercury	Stomach
Libra	Air	Cardinal	Venus	Pelvis
Scorpio	Water	Fixed	Mars (Pluto)	Genitalia
Sagittarius	Fire	Mutable	Jupiter	Thighs
Capricorn	Earth	Cardinal	Saturn	Knees
Aquarius	Air	Fixed	Saturn (Uranus)	Lower Legs
Pisces	Water	Mutable	Jupiter (Neptune)	Feet

APPENDIX 13

Dealing with Vexatious Elementals

Eliphas Levi gives instructions for dealing with troublesome elementals in his book *Transcendental Magic*, which is useful as a source, considering the potential for problems in dealing with the Elemental Kingdoms. We have adapted this to make it more functional.

Holding the Pentacle in one hand, and the dagger or sword in the other, recite the following conjuration in a loud voice:

Caput mortuum, the Lord command thee by the living and votive serpent! Cherub, the Lord command thee by Adam Kadmon! Wandering Eagle, the Lord command thee by the wings of the Bull! Serpent, the Lord Tetragrammaton command thee by the angel and the lion! Michael, Gabriel, Raphael and Uriel! Flow Moisture, by the Spirit of Elohim. Earth, be established by Jahveh. Spread, Firmament, by Jahveh Tzavaot. Fulfil, Judgement, by fire in the virtue of Michael. Angel of the blind eyes, obey, or pass away with this holy water! Work, Winged Bull, or revert to the earth, unless thou wilt that I should pierce thee with this sword! Chained Eagle, obey my sign, or fly before this breathing! Writhing Serpent, crawl at my feet, or be tortured by the sacred fire and give way before the perfumes that I burn in it! Water, return to water; fire, burn; air, circulate; earth, revert to earth, by virtue of the Pentagram, which is the Morning Star, and by the name of the Tetragrammaton, which is written in the centre of the Cross of Light! Amen.

Whilst this is going on, you should see a golden light spreading out from the pentacle, which pushes the elemental further away, causing it to become more intangible and insubstantial as it fades away and returns to its own elemental kingdom.

Terms and Definitions

A common problem in magick is misconceptions brought about by uncertainty and lack of clarity with regard to terms and definitions. If the context of terms is not used it can easily lead to confusion, defeating the purpose of the practices they describe. For the purpose of this book we are giving our definitions of terms we use and how they apply to the elemental work within.

- Hymn – a hymn is a spiritual song or lyrical religious poem, commonly used in adoration or praise of a deity. Hymns are normally recited to attract the attention of the deity, in the hope that they will add their power to your intent and ensure success. What we call a hymn is also known as a prayer, and is often referred to as invocation in modern pagan traditions, though by our definition this is not the case as the deity is not being called into something or someone as a visible image. Despite the name, a hymn does not include music, and when music is added to a hymn, it is the hymn tune. Examples of hymns of this kind are the Orphic Hymns to the Greek Gods. The hymns to the Elemental Gods within this book are based upon these Hymns in their style and content, rewritten in modern language.

- Invocation – is the process of calling a deity or spiritual creature into something or someone. This includes the use of crystal stones, glass receptacles, bowls of liquid and magick mirrors, statues as fetishes and techniques such as the Wiccan ceremony of *"Drawing Down the Moon"*, where a specific deity is called into a person who is awaiting this contact. The practical work with the elemental archangels found in the book is invocatory, being the calling of the archangels to appear within a crystal.

- Evocation - is the process of calling forth of a spiritual creature to tangible presence. When evocation is to visible appearance it is in a medium provided to give form to the creature, usually incense. It does not apply to the appearance of an image of the creature in a receptacle such as a crystal or mirror, which we have defined as invocation. Although we have not included any specific evocatory work in this book, we felt it appropriate to clarify the use of the term.

- Conjuration - refers to the calling of a spiritual creature, as part of the process of Invocation or Evocation. Although some old texts refer to the long prose calls as invocations, to avoid confusion we are using the term Conjuration to refer to this part of the process.

Bibliography

Agrippa, Henry Cornelius; *Three Books of Occult Philosophy*; 2005 (first published 1531); Llewellyn; Minnesota

----------; *Fourth Book of Occult Philosophy*; 1978 (first published 1565); Askin Press; London

Anon; *Harley MSS 5596*; 15C

----; *Sloane MSS 3825*; 1649

Ashe, Steven (ed); *The Testament of Solomon & The Wisdom of Solomon*; 2008; Glastonbury Books; Glastonbury

Barry, Kieren; *The Greek Qabalah*; 1999; Samuel Weiser Inc; Maine

Betz, Hans Dieter (ed); *The Greek Magical Papyri in Translation*; 1992; University of Chicago Press; Chicago

Bjerragard, C.H.A.; *The Elementals, The Elementary Spirits*; 1887; The Path

Briggs, Katharine; *A Dictionary of Fairies*; 1977; Penguin Books; London

Conway, David; *Magic: An Occult Primer*; 1972; Jonathan Cape Ltd; London

De Givry, Grillot; *Sorcery Magic and Alchemy*; 1991; Zachary Kwintner; London

Dennis, Rabbi Geoffrey W.; *The Encyclopedia of Jewish Myth, Magic and Mysticism*; 2007; Llewellyn; Minnesota

-----------; *The Use of Water as a Medium of Revelation in Early Jewish Mysticism*; 2008; in *Anthropology of Consciousness*, Vol 19.1:84-106

De Villars, Monfaucon; *The Count de Gabalis*; 1714 (English translation of the 1670 French work); B.Lintott & E. Curll; London

Evelyn-White, Hugh G. (trans); *Hesiod: The Homeric Hymns and Homerica*; 1914; LOEB; London

Feng, Gia-Fu & English, Jane (trans); *Tao Teh Ching*; 1973; Wildwood House; London

Forman, Simon; *Of the Division of Chaos*; Ashmole MS 240; 16C; Bodleian Library; Oxford

Fouqué, Friedrich de la Motte; *Undine*; 1909; William Heinemann; London

Galt, John; *The Bachelor's Wife*; 1824; Oliver & Boyd; Edinburgh

Gettings, Fred; *Dictionary of Occult, Hermetic & Alchemical Sigils*; 1981; Routledge and Kegan Paul; London

-----------; *The Arkana Dictionary of Astrology*; 1995; Penguin; London

Gjellerup, Karl; *Den Ældra Eddas Gudesange*; 1895; P.G. Philipsen; Copenhagen

Hall, Manly P.; *The Mystical and Medical Philosophy of Paracelsus*; 1964; The Philosophical Research Society Inc.; California

Hartmann, Franz; *Magic: White and Black*; 1888; George Redway; London

----------; *Paracelsus*; 1896; Kegan Paul; London

Hedegård, Gösta; *Liber Iuratus Honorii – A Critical Edition of the Latin Version of the Sworn Book of Honorius*; 2002; Almovist & Wiksell International; Stockholm

Heidel, Alexander; *The Babylonian Genesis*; 1963; University of Chicago Press; Chicago

James, King; *The Holy Bible*; 1785; R Crutwell; Bath

Kaplan, Aryeh; *Sefer Yetzirah: The Book of Creation*; 1997; Weiser Books; Minnesota

King, B.J.H. (trans); *The Grimoire of Pope Honorius III*; 1984; Sut Anubis Books; Northampton

King, Leonard W.; *Babylonian Magic and Sorcery*; 2000; Red Wheel Weiser; Maine

Kingsley, Peter; *Ancient Philosophy, Mystery and Magic; Empedocles and the Pythagorean Tradition*; 1995; Oxford University Press; Oxford

Kirk, G. S., Raven, J. E. & Schofield, M.; *The Presocratic Philosophers*; 1983; Cambridge University Press; Cambridge

Leland, Charles Godfrey; *Meister Karl's Sketch-book*; 1855; Parry & McMillan; Philadelphia

Lenormant, Francois; *Chaldean Magic: Its Origin and Development*; 1999 (first published 1878); Red Wheel Weiser; Maine

Levi, Eliphas; *Transcendental Magic*; 1979; Rider & Co; London

-----------; *The Magical Ritual of the Sanctum Regnum*; 1970; Crispin Press; London

Linden, Stanton J.; *The Alchemy Reader: From Hermes Trismegistus to Isaac Newton*; 2003; Cambridge University Press; Cambridge

McCurdy, Edward; *The Notebooks of Leonardo Da Vinci*; 1954; Plain Label Books

McLean, Adam (ed); *The Magical Calendar*; 1994, Panes Press; Michigan

Marathakis, Ioannis; *Anazetontas ten Kleida tou Solomonta*; 2007; Edikos Typos; Athens

Mathers, S.L. MacGregor; *The Key of Solomon the King (Clavicula Salomonis)*; 1976; Routledge & Kegan Paul; London

Mead, G.R.S.; *Thrice Greatest Hermes*; 2001; Samuel Weiser; Maine

Meyer, Marvin W. & Smith, Richard; *Ancient Christian Magic: Coptic Texts of Ritual Power*; 1999; Princeton University Press; Princeton

Mookerjee, Ajit & Khanna, Madhu; *The Tantric Way: Art, Science, Ritual*; 1977; Thames & Hudson; London

Paracelsus, Theophrastus; *Book of Nymphs, Sylphs, Pygmies, and Salamanders, and Kindred Beings*; 1616; Strassburg

----------; *Archidoxes of Magic*; 1976; Askin Press; London

Peterson, Joseph (ed); *The Sixth and Seventh Books of Moses*; 2008; Ibis Press; Florida

Philostratus & Jones, Christopher P.; *Life of Apollonius of Tyana*; 2005; LOEB; London

Pinch, Geraldine; *Egyptian Mythology*; 2002; Oxford University Press; Oxford

Rankine, David; *Climbing the Tree of Life: A Manual of Practical Magickal Qabalah*; 2005; Avalonia; London

Rankine, David, & d'Este, Sorita; *Practical Planetary Magick*; 2007, Avalonia; London

de Rola, Stanislas Klossowski; *The Golden Game: Alchemical Engravings of the Seventeenth Century*; 1997; Thames & Hudson; London

Roszak, Theodore; *Where the Wasteland Ends*; 1973; Bantam Doubleday Dell; New York

Rudd, Thomas; *Harley MSS 6482*; 17C; England

Schrödter, Willy; *A Rosicrucian Notebook*; 1992; Samuel Weiser Inc; Maine

Scott, Walter, *The Complete Works of Sir Walter Scott*; 1833; Conner & Cooke; New York

Shah, Sayed Idries; *The Secret Lore of Magic*; 1957; Frederick Muller; London

Skinner, Stephen; *The Complete Magician's Tables*; 2006; Golden Hoard Press; Singapore

Skinner, Stephen & Rankine, David; *The Keys to the Gateway of Magic*; 2005; Golden Hoard Press; Singapore

----------- & -----------; *The Goetia of Dr Rudd*; 2007; Golden Hoard Press; Singapore

----------- & -----------; *The Veritable Key of Solomon*; 2008; Holden Hoard Press; Singapore

Spence, Lewis; *Encyclopaedia of Occultism*; 2003; Courier Dover Publications; New York

Taylor, Thomas (trans); *The Hymns of Orpheus*; 1792; London

---------- (trans); *Iamblichus: On the Mysteries of the Egyptians, Chaldeans and Assyrians*; 1968 (originally 1821); Stuart & Watkins; London

----------- (trans); *Fragments that Remain of the Lost Writings of Proclus*; 1825; sacred-texts.com

Thorndike, Lynn; *A History of Magic and Experimental Science*; 1958; Columbia University Press; Columbia

Trithemius, Abbot Johannes; *Liber Octo Questionum*; 1515; Hasselbergen; Oppenheim

Waddell, W. (trans); *Manetho*; 1964; William Heinemann Ltd; London

Walsh, Patrick Gerard (trans), & Cicero, Marcus Tullius; *The Nature of the Gods*; 1997; Oxford University Press; Oxford

Westcott. W. Wynn (ed); *The Chaldean Oracles of Zoroaster*; 1983; The Aquarian Press; Northampton

Williams, J.F.C. (trans); *Aristotle: De Generatione et Corruptione*; 1982; Oxford University Press; Oxford

Wright, M.R.; *Empedocles: The Extant Fragments*; 1981; Yale University Press; London

Wunsch, R (ed); *De Mensibus*; 1898; Teuber; Leipzig

LaVergne, TN USA
02 September 2010
195668LV00004B/24/P